Dictionary of Physics

Dictionary of Physics

Taniya Sachdeva

Published by
PRABHAT PRAKASHAN PVT. LTD.
4/19 Asaf Ali Road,
New Delhi-110 002 (INDIA)
e-mail: prabhatbooks@gmail.com

ISBN 978-93-5048-513-2
DICTIONARY OF PHYSICS
by Taniya Sachdeva

Edition
2025

Price
₹ 450.00 (Rupees Four Hundred Fifty only)

Printed at
Narula Printers, Delhi

To Albert Einstein

Preface

Physics or the science of nature is a vast study which involves matter, motion through space and time. It also deals with energy and force. Physics is one of the oldest sciences. It has aroused the interest of many scientists through the ages who have tried to explain its various aspects in their innumerable researches. The terminology used by them is very complex and not so easy to understand. To a student of physics the terms used to throw light on the different aspects of physics may be familiar but are often confusing and the meaning not always clear. Therefore while studying physics the students need to understand the precise meaning of the terms in order to comprehend the concept. This book caters to this need.

This book is one of a series of dictionaries designed for school students and to be used in schools to help understand the terms of Physics and better comprehend them. It will also be of great help to other science students and those interested in science.

In today's society, where education should be and is at the forefront, a book of this kind will not only captivate a young mind but also enable parents to respond to the incessant queries of their children and help whet their curiosity. This dictionary deals extensively with Physics terms and will provide readers an instant access to the specialised knowledge of words relating to physics in a way that is lucid, informative and easy to understand.

Like the other sciences physics too is not confined to a water tight compartment nor is its boundaries rigidly defined. It intersects other areas and is linked with other sciences. New ideas are developing with further research taking place. Thus the concepts are constantly changing. Technology is also developing with theoretical breakthroughs. Therefore new terminology has evolved keeping pace with new development of concepts and alteration of old. This often leads to confusion and one needs to refer to a book for clarification.

This dictionary has been specially written keeping this in mind. It covers the recent developments in Physics and other sciences related to Physics which will help readers to keep abreast with the recent developments in the field of Physics. Those interested in physics purely for knowledge sake and to keep pace with technology will find this book a great help. It will definitely be a treat for those who consult it.

Besides this the classic (which includes the traditional form) and modern concepts of physics have been dealt extensively.

In this Dictionary of Physics the central ideas and concepts of the terms are methodically explained. Each term is first defined briefly and then explained very clearly. Its aim is to offer an intensive and extensive meaning of the word including their changing implications. Cross-references are given in italics which help clarify concepts as well as lead to further interpretations of the terms.

This dictionary will definitely be helpful to all - students, teachers, parents and those with insatiable curiosity and urge to gain more knowledge.

Acknowledgement

I am thankful to the Almighty for giving me strength to write this work and many other books that I have authored so far.

I am equally grateful to my loving and caring parents, who have nurtured me to face the complexities of life.

My respected teachers have always been an inspiration, helping me be what I am today.

Contents

Aberration

It is an optical phenomenon in which a lens or mirror fails to produce a good image.

Absolute

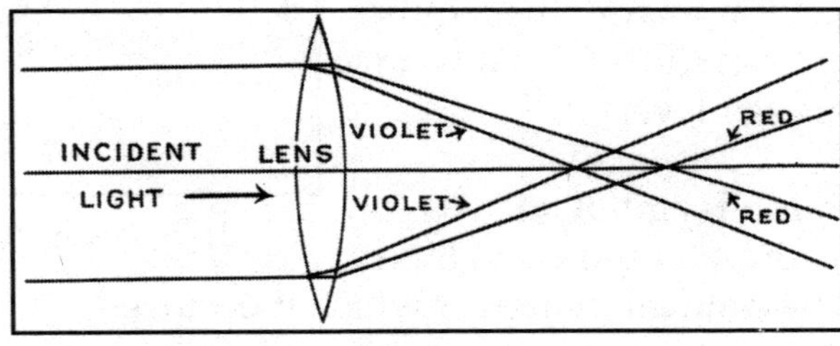

Aberration

This refers to something that is perfect or complete or pure; something that is not relative.

Absolute temperature

It is another name for thermodynamic temperature, which is measured on an absolute scale (Celsius or Fahrenheit).

Absolute zero

Through the means of thermodynamics, it is the temperature at which molecular motion stops and reaches the zero point (0°K, or –273.15°C, or –459.67°F) on the absolute temperature scale.

Absorption

A process in which one substance permeates another; for instance, a gas dissolved by a liquid or solid, or a fluid permeated by a liquid or solid.

Absorption coefficient

Also known as molar absorption coefficient, it is a measure of the rate denoting the intensity of electro-magnetic radiation as light, as it passes through a substance or material.

Absorption spectrum

It is a spectrum related to the absorption of electro-magnetic radiation by atoms or other entities resulting from shifts from lower to higher energy levels.

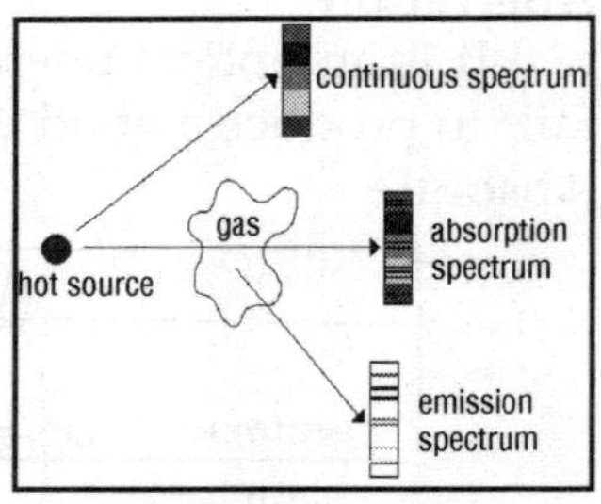

Absorption spectrum

Acceleration [symbol: a]

It is the change in velocity divided by time interval over which it occurred.

Accelerator

It is a device used for increasing or speeding up the kinetic energies of particles which are charged.

Acceptor

Another name for acceptor impurity, this is a substance which when added in a semiconducting crystal obtains one or more electrons.

Accumulator

It is a kind of secondary cell or storage battery, which is recharged by passing electric current through it from an external direct current supply. During this process, the chemical reactions in the cell are reversed by the charging current. Some examples are the lead-acid accumulator, the nickel-cadmium cell, etc.

Accuracy

It is the closeness of a measurement to the standard value of that quantity.

Achromatic lens

It is a type of lens for which all light colours have the same focal length.

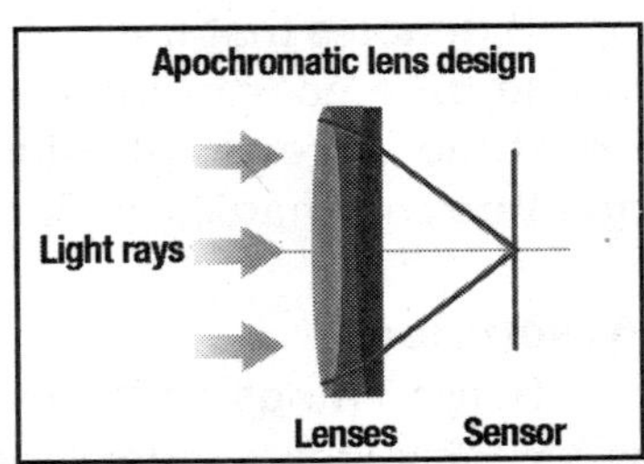

Achromatic lens

Acoustics

It is the branch of physics concerning the study of the properties of sound and sound waves.

Actinium [Ac]

The atomic number of this soft, silvery-white radioactive chemical element is 89. It is rarely found as in uranium ores as an impurity. It has found its uses in medicine, and is a source of alpha rays.

Actinometer

It is a device for measuring the intensity of radiation, usually electromagnetic radiation.

Active device

These are products containing electronic components such as transistors, integrated circuits and vacuum tubes, need an external power source for performing an action.

Activity [symbol: a]

It is a thermodynamic function that in a non-ideal

solution denotes the effective concentration of dissolved matter.

Adhesion

It is the force of attraction between two unlike materials.

Adiabatic approximation

It denotes that the solution of the Schrödinger equation at one time goes uninterruptedly over to the solution at a later time. An example of adiabatic approximation, used in quantum mechanics, is Born-Oppenheimer approximation.

Adsorption

Synonymous with surface assimilation, this takes place when there is an accumulation of gases, liquids on the surface of a solid or liquid.

Adsorption isotherm

It is an illustration of the connection between the bulk activity of adsorbate and the amount adsorbed at constant temperature.

Aerodynamics

It is the branch of mechanics concerning the motion of air and its effects of the interaction between the air and solid bodies moving through it.

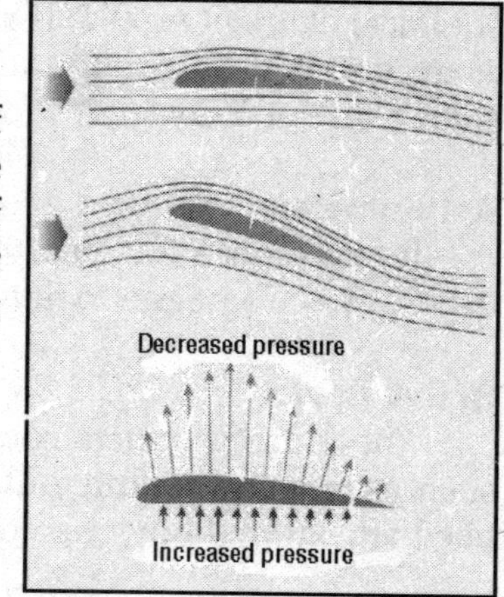

Aerodynamics

Aerosol

It is a cloud of solid or liquid particles suspended in gas.

Aerospace

It refers to the atmosphere of the earth and the outer space.

Air

A mixture of many gases, mainly of oxygen and nitrogen, this invisible gas surrounds the earth.

Air resistance

It is the force of air on objects moving through it.

Alloy

This metal is made by a combination of two or more metallic (or non-metallic) elements; for instance, steel is an alloy of iron and carbon.

Alpha decay

It is a process in which a nucleus emits an alpha particle.

Alpha particle

It is a positively charged particle in the helium nucleus, which is emitted by some radioactive materials.

Alternating current

Used in power supplies, this electric current, abbreviated as AC, reverses its course several times a second at regular intervals.

Alternator

This generator is an electromechanical device that uses mechanical energy to produce electrical energy in the form of alternating current.

Altimeter

It is an instrument for measuring the altitude and is used as a barometric or radar device in navigation.

Altimeter

Americium [Am]

This chemical element is produced by

the beta decay of an isotope of plutonium. It is a radioactive metal of the actinide series with atomic number as 95.

Ammeter

It is an instrument for measuring electrical current.

Amorphous

It refers to something which is not crystalline, and does not have a definite form or structure.

Amount of substance [symbol: n]

It is a standard quantity that measures the size of a specified group of elementary entities, such as atoms, molecules, electrons, etc.

Ampere [symbol: A]

It is a unit of electrical current; 1 ampere equals 1 coulomb per second.

Amplifier

This electronic equipment is used for changing or increasing the amplitude of electrical signals passing through it.

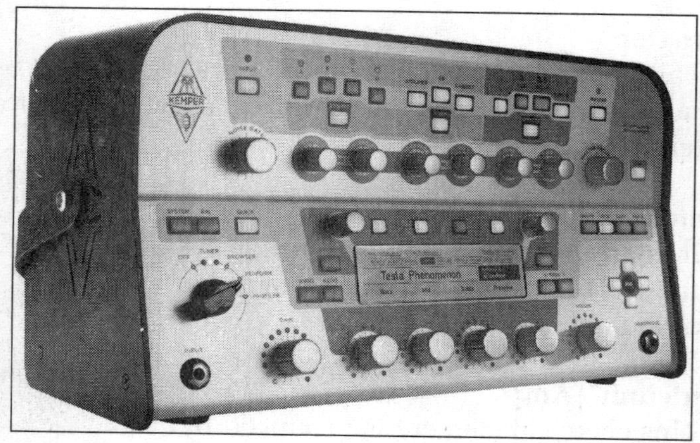

Amplifier

Amplitude

It refers to the maximum displacement from equilibrium in any periodic motion.

Anastigmatic lens

This is a photographic lens completely corrected for spherical aberration, coma and astigmatism.

Anemometer

It is a device for determining the speed of the wind, or measuring any gas current.

Angle of reflection

It is the angle between direction of motion of waves and a line perpendicular to surface the waves are reflected from.

Angle of refraction

It is the angle between direction of motion of waves and a line perpendicular to surface the waves are refracted from.

Angular momentum

It is the quantity of rotational motion, for instance, for a rotating object, it is the product of moment of inertia and angular velocity.

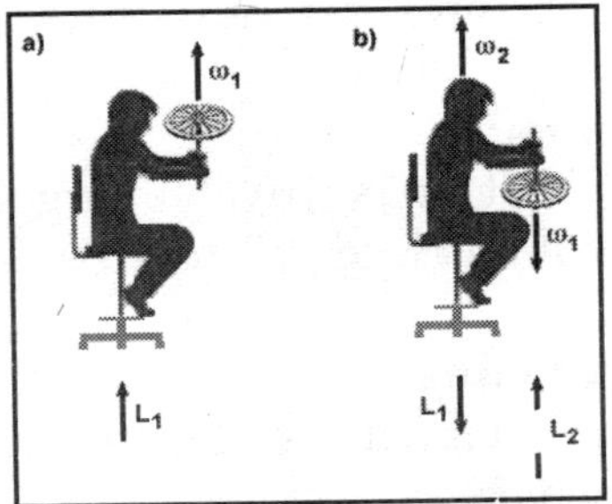

Angular momentum

Anharmonic oscillator

Used in classical or quantum mechanics, it is an oscillator that is not oscillating in simple harmonic motion.

Anhydrous

A substance is anhydrous if it has little water or is waterless.

Anion

It is (i) a negative ion; (ii) atom or group of atoms that has gained one or more electrons.

Annealing

It is a heat treatment in which a metal is altered, resulting in the changes in its properties such as strength and hardness.

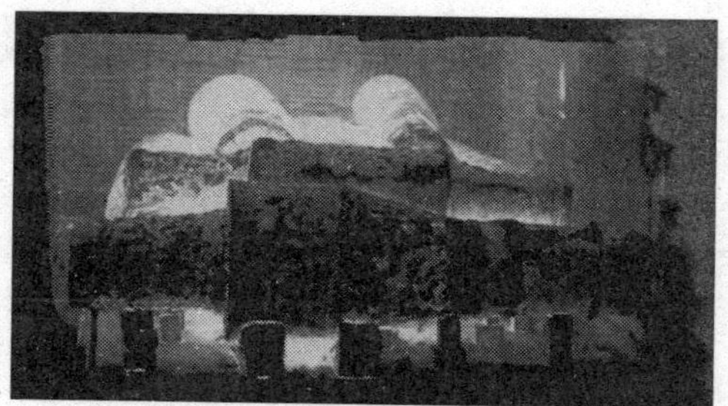

Annealing

Annihilation

It is the process in which a particle and its antiparticle are converted into energy.

Anode

It is a positively charged electrode by which the electrons exit an electrical device.

Antenna

It is a device used to receive or transmit electromagnetic waves.

Antiatom

It refers to any atom made of antiparticles.

Antineutrino

It is a subatomic particle with no charge or mass emitted in beta decay.

Antinode

It is the point of maximum displacement of two superimposed waves.

Aperture

It is a hole or an opening through which light travels or passes in an optical or photographic instrument.

Aqueous

It relates to, or is similar to, or contains water (generally as solvent or medium).

Archimedes' principle

It states that an object immersed in a fluid has an upward force equal to the weight of the fluid displaced by the object.

Astatine

Occurring in traces in nature as a decay product, it is a highly unstable radioactive element of the halogen group with its atomic number as 85.

Asteroids

It refers to small celestial bodies made of rock and metal that move around the sun.

Asteroids

Astronomy

It is the branch of physics concerning celestial objects, space, and the physical universe as a whole.

Astrophysics

It is the branch of astronomy related to the physical and chemical properties and nature of stars and other celestial bodies.

Atmolysis

It is a technique of separating a mixture of gases with different densities.

Atom

It is the smallest particle of an element.

Atomic bomb

This weapon is an explosive force that derives its power from nuclear fission.

Atomic mass unit

Also called unified mass unit or the dalton, it is a unit used for denoting atomic and formula weights. It is one-twelfth of a mass of an atom of the carbon-12 isotope.

Atomic number

It is the integral number of protons in the nucleus, and also defines the identity of element.

Atomic weight

Also known as relative atomic mass, it is the weighted average of the masses of the constituent isotopes of an element.

Audibility

It refers to the range of sound-wave frequencies that are audible to humans, ranging from 30 to 20,000 Hertz.

Audiometer

It is a device used for measuring the hearing ability or evaluating hearing loss.

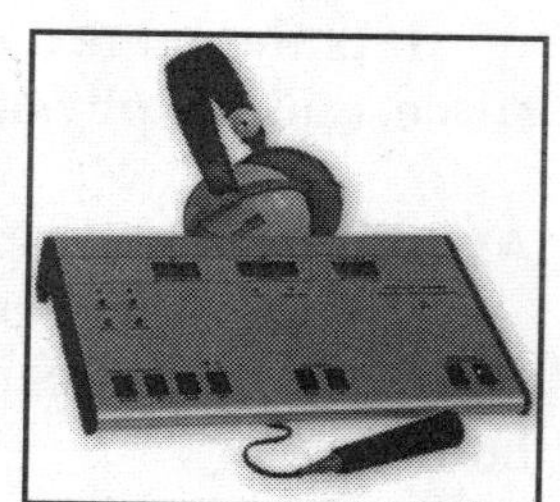

Audiometer

Aurora

An atmospheric phenomenon consisting of bands of light caused by charged solar particles following the earth's magnetic lines of force.

Austentite

Constituent of some steel forms, this solid solution of carbon in a non-magnetic form of iron is stable at high temperatures.

Avalanche

It is a phenomenon in which a fast-moving ions or electrons collide with each other producing further ions and electrons.

Average velocity

It is the velocity measured over a finite time interval.

Avionics

Referring to a combination of aviation and electronics, it is the science and technology of electronic systems and devices for aeronautics and astronautics including communications, navigation and guidance, etc.

Avionics

Avogadro's law

Also known as Avogadro's hypothesis, here at the same temperature and pressure, equal volumes of all gases have the same number of molecules.

Azeotrope

Also known as azeotropic mixture, it is a solution (mixture) of two liquids that has a constant boiling point and composition during distillation.

□

Babbitt metal

Also called bearing metal, this soft, white alloy of tin with some copper and antimony is used in bearings to reduce friction

Babo's law

Named after Lambert von Babo, it is a law which states that the vapour pressure of a solution is lowered in proportion to the amount of solute added.

Back e.m.f.

Also known as the counter-electromotive force, it is the voltage force that pushes against the current which induces it.

Background radiation

This uniform microwave radiation remaining from the Big Bang is extraneous to an experiment.

Balance

It is a device for weighing, such as the simple beam balance (a central pivot, beam and a pair of scales).

Balance

Ballistic galvanometer

It is a type of mirror galvanometer in which a moving-coil galvanometer with a long swing period is used for measuring electric charge in a current pulse.

Ballistic pendulum

It is an instrument for measuring a bullet's momentum which allows direct calculation and measurement of the projectile velocity and kinetic energy.

Ballistics

It is the science of flight dynamics and mechanics of projectiles and firearms, related to the flight, behaviour, and effects of projectiles, gravity bombs, rockets, etc.

Ball lightning

Usually associated with thunderstorms, it is a rare and little known atmospheric electrical phenomenon having the form of lightning in the shape of a glowing red ball (consisting of ionized gas) that can last from a few seconds to some minutes.

Ball lightning

Band theory

It is the theory explaining electrical conduction in solids.

Bandwidth

It refers to the range of frequencies within a given band used for transmitting a signal through which a system or a device can operate effectively.

Barograph

It is kind of barometer that automatically records the variations in atmospheric pressure and its readings on a moving chart or sheet or rotating drum.

Barometer

It is a device for measuring atmospheric pressure and is used in forecasting the weather and determining altitude.

Barycentre

It refers to the mass center which is the mean location of all the mass in a system.

Barye [symbol: Ba]

It is a unit of pressure under the CGS system. It is equal to 1 dyne per square centimetre (1 Ba = 0.1 Pa = 0.1 N/m^2)

Baryon

This subatomic particle made of three quarks interacts with the strong nuclear force.

Battery

It is an arrangement of two or more cells electrically connected together to generate electric energy.

Baud [symbol: Bd]

Usually associated with telecommunications and electronics, it is a unit used to express the speed of transmission of electronic signals and is synonymous to symbols per second or pulses per second.

Beam

It is a group of electromagnetic radiation or particles that can produce a visual sensation.

Beam

Beat

It refers to the slow oscillation in amplitude of a complex wave.

Beckmann thermometer

Named after Ernst Otto Beckmann, it is a limited range mercury thermometer with a large bulb which is used to measure small differences of temperature with great precision, but not absolute temperature values.

Becquerel [symbol: Bq]

It is the SI unit of radioactivity, where one Bq is defined as the activity of a quantity of radioactive material in which one nucleus decays per second.

Bell metal

This hard alloy of bronze, copper and tin is used in maufacturing bells.

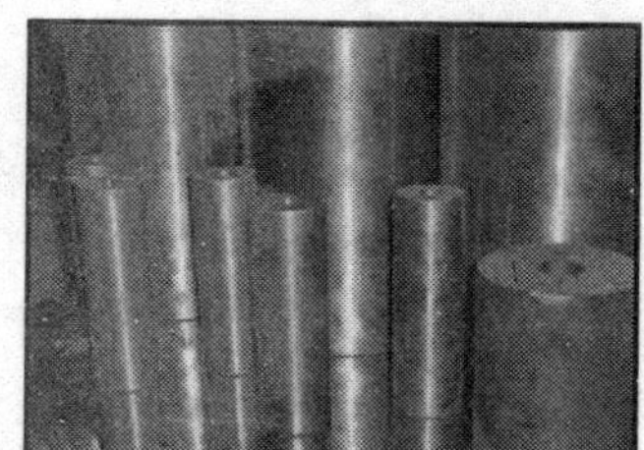

Bell metal

Berkelium [Bk]

The atomic number of this radioactive metal is 97. This transuranic element of the actinide series was first created artificially by bombarding americium with helium ions.

Bernoulli's principle

This principle states that when a fixed quantity of fluid flows, the pressure is decreased when the flow velocity increases.

Beta decay

It is a radioactive decay process in which an electron or positron and neutrino are emitted from a nucleus.

Beta iron

Similar to alpha iron, it is a non-magnetic allotrope of pure iron which remains stable between 770°C and 910°C.

Beta particle

It is the electron emitted from the nucleus when a neutron decays to a proton and an electron.

Betatron

It is a particle accelerator that is used to accelerate electrons in a circular path by magnetic induction with a target of generating high energy radiation.

Biconcave

It refers to the quality of a material (especially an optical lens) in which both the surfaces, front and back, are concave.

Big-bang theory

It is the theory stating that the origin of the universe was sometime between 10 billion and 20 billion years ago, and it happened from the cataclysmic explosion of a small volume of matter at extremely high density and temperature.

Bimetallic strip

It is a temperature-sensitive strip consisting of two metals which bends with a rise in temperature, and is, therefore, used in some thermostats.

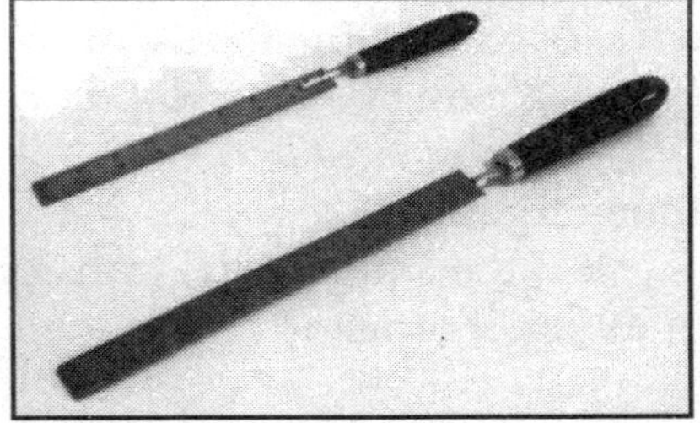

Bimetallic strip

Bimorph cell

It is a cell in which two piezoelectric crystals joined together so that an applied voltage results in expansion of one and contraction of the other, transforming electrical signals into mechanical energy. It is mainly used in loudspeakers, gramophone pick-ups, etc.

Binary stars

It is a star-system of two stars, primary (brighter) and secondary, in which one star revolves around the other or both revolve around a common center of mass under their mutual gravitation.

Binding energy

It is the negative of the amount of energy needed to separate a nucleus into individual nucleons.

Binoculars

Also called field glasses or binocular telescopes, it is an optical instrument with a lens for both eyes, and is used for seeing objects at a distance.

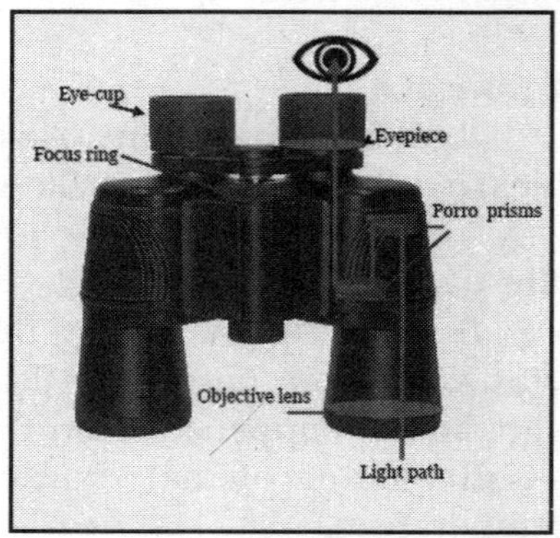

Binoculars

Binocular vision

It refers to the vision involving the use of both eyes with overlapping fields of view, allowing good perception of depth and range of vision.

Bioenergetics

It is the study of the transformation and flow of energy in living organisms.

Bioluminescence

It is the biochemical production and emission of light by physiological processes in living organisms, such as fireflies and deep-sea fishes.

Biomechanics

It is the study of the mechanical laws and principles concerning the movement or structure of living organisms, such as humans, animals, plants.

Biophysics

It is the branch of science in which the laws of physics are applied to biological phenomena and problems.

Biotechnology

It is the study of molecular biology (micro-organisms), where such knowledge can be used to perform specific industrial processes.

Biprism

It refers to an optical instrument in which two prisms of very acute angle are placed side by side, and is used on the screens of cameras.

Bit

It is a unit of measurement of information in computing and telecommunications referred to as either a 0 or 1 in binary notation.

Black body

This hypothetical object can absorb all electromagnetic radiation falling on it and can also incandescently re-emit radiation.

Black hole

It is a region of space resulting from the deformation of spacetime caused by a very compact mass. It has an extremely high gravitational field, and is so intense that no matter or radiation can escape.

Black hole

Blooming

It is a process of accumulating and coating (usually a lens) with a thin layer of a substance, often magnesium fluoride, to remove surface reflection.

Bohrium [Bh]

Created artificially by high-energy atomic collisions, it is an unstable, transuranic chemical element with its atomic number as 107.

Boiling point

Also called condensation point, it is the temperature at which the vapour pressure of a liquid is equal to the applied pressure.

Bolometer

It is a sensitive electrical device for measuring radiant energy or the energy of incident electromagnetic radiation.

Bomb calorimeter

It is a strong sealed vessel made of a corrosion-resistant alloy and is mainly used for measuring heat of combustion.

Bomb calorimeter

Born-Haber cycle

It is a chain of reactions which, when summed, denotes the hypothetical one-step reaction by which elements in their standard states are converted into crystals of ionic compounds.

Boron counter tube

A proportional counter tube filled with boron fluoride or having electrodes coated with boron or boron compounds for detecting and counting neutrons.

Boson

It is a subatomic particle that has zero or integral spin and obeys the statistical description given by Bose and Einstein, but not the Pauli's exclusion principle.

Bosonisation

It is (i) the act, process or result of bosonizing; (ii) a mathematical procedure by which a system of interacting fermions in (1+1) dimensions can be transformed to a system of massless, non-interacting bosons.

Bound state

It defines a system where a particle or a body is subject to a potential in a way that it tends to remain localised in one or more regions of space.

Boyle's law

The law in which at constant temperature, the volume occupied by a definite mass of a gas is inversely proportional to the applied pressure.

Brass

It is a class of various metal alloys made chiefly of copper and zinc.

Brass

Breakdown

It is a sudden excessive increase in current through an insulating medium when medium fails to withstand an applied electric field.

Breeder reactor

It is a nuclear reactor that generates more fissionable nuclear fuel or material at a faster rate than it consumes.

Brinell hardness

Synonymous with the Brinell scale, it refers to the relative hardness of metals and alloys measured through the scale of penetration of an indenter, loaded on a material test-piece.

Britannia metal

Also called britannium, it is a silvery, pewter-kind alloy with a smooth surface, which consists of tin, antimony and some copper.

Broadband

Related to the field of telecommunications, it refers to a network in which multiple signals are used over a wide range of frequencies in high-capacity telecommunications, such as the Internet.

Bronze

It is a yellowish-brown-coloured alloy of copper with one-third tin (approx.) and is used for industrial and aesthetic purposes.

Brown dwarf

It is a celestial, sub-stellar object which is too low in mass to sustain stable hydrogen fusion. It is between a giant planet and a small star in size, and is believed to emit mainly infrared radiation.

Brush

It is a kind of electrical contact which conducts current between rotating and stationary parts of a generator or motor.

Bubble chamber

It is an instrument containing superheated liquid in which the path of ionizing particles is made visible as trails of tiny bubbles.

Bubble chamber

Buckminsterfullerene [C_{60}]

It is a form of carbon containing molecules of 60 atoms organised in a polyhedron similar to a geodesic sphere.

Bumping

It is a phenomenon in which a solvent becomes overheated, resulting in a sudden release of a vapour bubble, driving liquid to flow out of the flask in an explosive manner.

Bunsen cell

This early electrical battery is a zinc-carbon primary cell made of zinc and graphite in dilute chromic acid.

Buoyant force

It refers to the upward force on an object immersed in fluid.

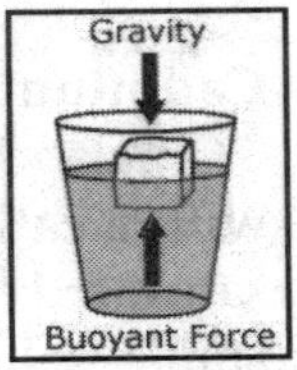

Buoyant force

Byte

It is an ordered collection of binary digits or bits (usually eight) operated on as a unit of digital information in computing and telecommunications.

□

C

Cadmium cell

Also known as the Weston cell, it is a wet-chemical cell with a cathode of cadmium amalgam and an electrolyte of saturated cadmium sulfate solution, which produces a highly stable voltage used as a standard in laboratories.

Caesium clock

Synonymous with an atomic clock, it is based on the energy difference between two states of the caesium nucleus in a magnetic field.

Caesium clock

Calculus

It is the branch of mathematics that deals with limits and with the differentiation and integration of functions.

Californium [Cf]

This synthetic, transuranic, radioactive metallic element in the actinide series, with its atomic number as 9, is used mainly as a neutron emitter.

Calomel half cell

Also known as calomel electrode, it is a reference electrode containing mercury, mercurous chloride and potassium chloride, and is used in electrometric measurement of acidity, voltammetry, etc.

Caloric theory

It is a scientific theory, now obsolete, which states that heat has a fluid called caloric that moves from hotter to colder bodies or zones.

Calorie

It can refer to (i) the energy needed to raise the temperature of 1 gram of water through 1 °C (defined as 4.1868 joules); (ii) food contains energy, which is measured in calories or kcalories (1,000 calories = 1 kcalorie).

Calorimeter

It is a device used to assess the heat transfer between system and surroundings.

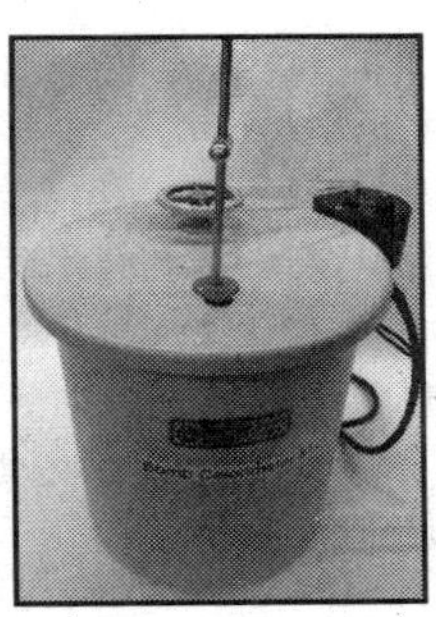

Calorimeter

Camcorder

This electronic device is a portable combined video camera and video recorder into one unit, which is used for recording images and audio on to a storage device.

Camera

It is a device for recording photographs, movie film, or video signals, comprising a lightproof box with a lens at one end and light-sensitive film at the other.

Canada balsam

Obtained from the balsam fir, it is a yellowish resin used for mounting preparations on microscope slides.

Yellow transparent exudate of the balsam fir; used as a transparent cement in optical devices (especially in microscopy) and as a mounting medium balsam fir: medium-sized fir of north-eastern North America; leaves smell of balsam when crushed; much used for pulpwood and Christmas trees.

Canada balsam, also called Canada turpentine or balsam of fir, is a turpentine which is made from the resin of the balsam fir tree.

Candela [symbol: Cd]

It is the SI unit of luminous intensity.

Capacitance

It is the ratio of charge stored per increase in potential difference.

Capacitor

It is an electrical device used to store charge and energy in the electrical field.

Capillary

It is a tube that has a small inside diameter.

Capillary

Capillary action

It is the rise of liquid in narrow tube due to surface tension.

Capture

It is any phenomenon in which an atomic or nuclear system acquires or absorbs an additional atomic or subatomic particle.

Carat

Abbreviated as ct or kt, it is a unit of mass equal to 200 mg (0.007055 oz), which is used for measuring gold, gemstones and pearls.

Carbon dating

Also called radiocarbon dating, it is a chemical analysis in which there is a determination of the age of an organic object from the relative proportions of the carbon isotopes carbon-12 and carbon-14 that it consists.

Carbon fibres

Another name for a composite, this typically gloss-black material contains extremely thin, strong crystalline fibres of carbon, and is used as a strengthening material in resins and ceramics.

Carbon fibres

Carnot efficiency

It is the ideal efficiency of heat engine or refrigerator working between two constant temperatures.

Carrier gas

In gas chromatography, it is the mobile phase in which a gas (helium, nitrogen, argon or hydrogen) continuously flows from a pressurized source through the column, transporting components of the sample with it.

Carrier wave

Also called carrier, it is a high-frequency electromagnetic wave that can be modulated in amplitude or frequency to transmit a signal or information in telecommunications.

Cartesian coordinates

It refers to a mathematical representation of Euclidean space in which the point whose location in space is denoted in terms of its distance above or below an X, a Y and a Z coordinate plane, and the point (0, 0, 0) is called the origin.

Cascade liquefier

It is an instrument used to liquefy air or oxygen, etc.

Cascade process

It refers to any process that occurs in a number of steps to produce the desired end result or product.

Case hardening

Another name for surface hardening, it is a special heat-treatment process of hardening the surface of a metal by infusing elements into the material's surface, forming a thin layer of a harder alloy.

Cast iron

It is an alloy of iron and carbon, which has more carbon than steel. This hard, heavy, brittle, unchangeable metal is formed by casting in moulds, and is used for architectural purposes.

Cast iron

Catalytic converter

It is an antipollution device on an automotive system containing a platinum-iridium catalyst for converting pollutant gases into less harmful ones and reducing the toxicity of emissions.

Catastrophe theory

It is a branch of mathematics referring to the bifurcation theory concerned with dynamical systems exhibiting abrupt discontinuous alterations.

Cathetometer

This optical instrument is used for measuring vertical distances in cases not going beyond a few decimeters.

Cathode

It is an electrode at which reduction takes place.

Cathode rays

It is a negatively charged beam of electrons that are emitted by the cathode of a high-vacuum tube or an electrical discharge tube.

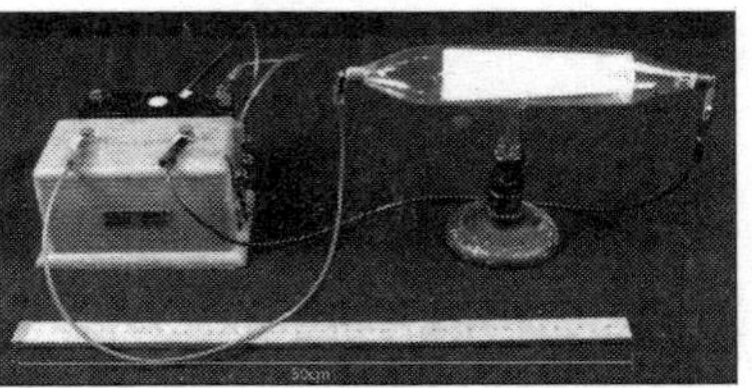

Cathode rays

Cathode ray tube

It is a closed glass tube which has a gas under low pressure, and produces cathode rays when high voltage is applied.

Cation

It is (i) a positive ion; (ii) an atom or group of atoms that has lost one or more electrons.

Causality

It is the principle referring to the relationship between the cause (first event) and the effect (second event), where the second event is a consequence of the first.

Cavitation

It is a process in which vapour bubbles are formed in a flowing liquid due to the extreme reduction of pressure on the back of the propeller blade.

CD

An abbreviation of Compact Disc, it is a digitally encoded recording on an optical disc used to store digital data and is played back by a laser.

CD-ROM

It is a compact disc used as a read-only optical memory device for a computer system.

CD-RW

It is a blank compact disc that can be recorded, erased, and rerecorded many times.

Cell

It is a device that has electrodes immersed in an electrolyte, and is utilised for producing electric current.

Celestial mechanics

It is the branch of theoretical astronomy concerning with the calculation and application of Newton's laws of the motions of heavenly bodies.

Celestial sphere

Related to astronomy and navigation, it is an imaginary sphere of which the observer is the center and on which all celestial objects appear to be projected.

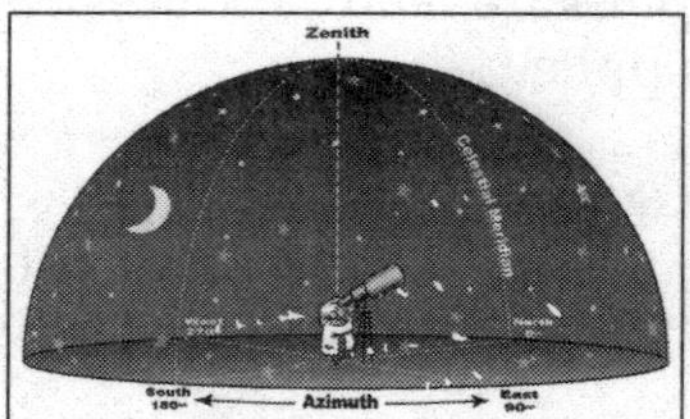

Celestial sphere

Celsius scale

Named after Anders Celsius, it is a temperature scale in which the freezing point of water is 0° and the boiling point of water is 100°.

Cementation

This process involves the impregnation (part of plastination) of the surface of a metal with another material by means of high-temperature diffusion.

Cementite [Fe_3C]

Also called iron carbide, it is a hard, brittle compound of iron and carbon and is a constituent of cast iron and most steels.

Centi-

It is a term used typically in units of measurement referring to one hundredth.

Centrifugal force

It is the force that seems to draw a rotating body away from the centre of rotation.

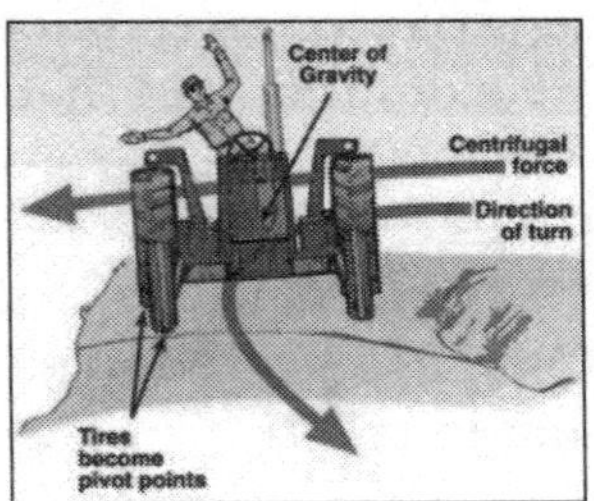

Centrifugal force

Centripetal force

It is a force that causes centripetal acceleration.

Cermet

It is a class of composite, heat-resistant materials made of ceramic and sintered metal with the properties of both ceramics and metals, which is used mainly as a thermal spray material.

CERN

Known as the European Organization for Nuclear Research, it is the world's largest particle physics laboratory which was established in 1954.

Cetane number

It is a measure of the combustion quality of diesel fuel relative to cetane as a standard during compression ignition.

c.g.s. units

Known as the Centimetre-Gram-Second System, it is a metric system of physical units where centimetre is a unit of length, gram is a unit of mass, and second is a unit of time.

Chain reaction

This reaction, in which reactive species are produced in more than one step, when started, sustains itself and expands.

Chaos

It can refer to (i) the dynamical system that is extremely

sensitive to its conditions in the beginning; (ii) the disordered state of unformed matter and infinite space.

Charge carrier

It refers to a mobile particle carrying an electric charge that passes through electrical conductors, such as electrons and ions.

Charged

It denotes an object that has an unbalance of positive and negative electrical charges.

Charging by conduction

It is a process of charging by touching neutral object to a charged object.

Charging by induction

It is a phenomenon of charging by bringing neutral object near charged object, then removing part of resulting separated charge.

Charle's law

This law states that at constant pressure, the volume occupied by a definite mass of gas is directly proportional to its absolute temperature.

Chemical dating

It is a technique in which measuring the chemical compositions helps to ascertain the age of minerals (relative or absolute) and of ancient objects.

Chip

In electronics, it is a small slice of semiconducting material, also called microchip, which is cut from a larger wafer of the material.

Chip

Chirality

It implies a phenomenon in which an object varies from its mirror image, having different left-handed and right-handed forms.

Choke

It is an electrical inductor in the form of an inductance coil with low resistance and high inductance used in electrical circuits to smoothen the variations of AC current.

Chromatic aberration

It is variation in focal length of lens with wavelength of light.

Chromium steel

Synonymous with stainless steel, it is the steel consisting of chromium making it corrosion-resistant.

Chromosphere

It is a reddish gaseous layer or portion above the photosphere of the sun that can be seen during a total eclipse of the sun, and comprising transparent ionized hydrogen and helium at 4000° to 40,000°C.

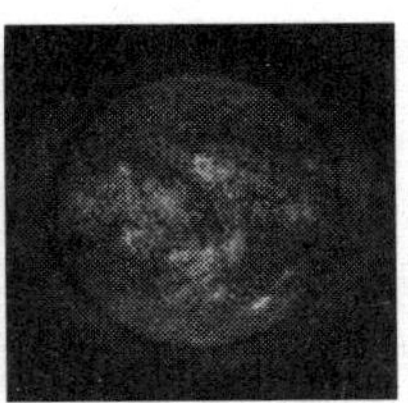

Chromosphere

Circle

It is a round plane figure whose circumference has points equidistant from a fixed point which is the center.

Circular motion

It is the motion with constant radius of curvature caused by acceleration being perpendicular to velocity.

Cladding

It is the covering or coating of one structure or material with another.

Clark cell

Named after Josiah Latimer Clark, it is a form of voltaic cell or wet-chemical cell which is used as a laboratory standard.

Claude process

It is a phenomenon of ammonia synthesis which makes use of high-operating pressures and a train of converters.

Clock reading

It is the time between event and a reference time which is usually zero.

Close packing

It refers to the manner in which atoms are packed and arranged in a crystal occupying the least amount of physical space.

Close packing

Closed-isolated system

It denotes a grouping of objects in a way that neither matter nor energy can come in or go out of the collection.

Closed-pipe resonator

It is a cylindrical tube with one end closed and a sound source at the other end.

Cloud chamber

Another name for Wilson chamber, it is an apparatus containing air or gas supersaturated with water or alcohol vapour is used to detect high-energy charged particles, X-rays, and gamma rays, etc.

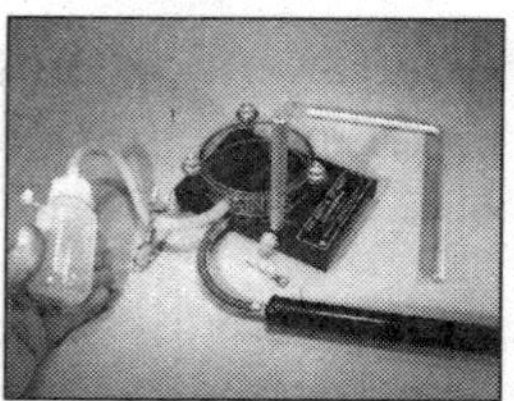

Cloud chamber

Coagulation

It is (i) the conversion from a liquid to a semisolid state; (ii) the precipitation of suspended colloidal particles by the means of physical or chemical processes.

Coal

Found in underground deposits, it is a readily combustible fossil fuel in the form of black or dark brown rock consisting mainly of carbonized plant matter, and is mainly used as fuel.

Cobalt steel

It is a hard alloy which is one of the variations of high speed steel consisting of more cobalt in it, and is used to drill strong materials.

Coefficient

In mathematics, it is a numerical or constant quantity placed before and multiplying the variable in an algebraic expression.

Coefficient of friction

It refers to the ratio of frictional force and the normal force between two forces.

Coefficient of linear expansion

It is the alteration in length divided by original length and by temperature change.

Coefficient of volume expansion

It is the alteration in volume divided by original volume and by temperature change.

Coelostat

This optical instrument has a rotating and fixed mirror that constantly reflects the light from the same area of sky. This updated version of heliostat is used mainly to track the path of a celestial body.

Coherent waves

These are waves in which all are in step or in phase.

Cohesive force

It refers to the attractive force between similar substances.

Coincidence circuit

It is an electronic instrument with one output and two or more inputs.

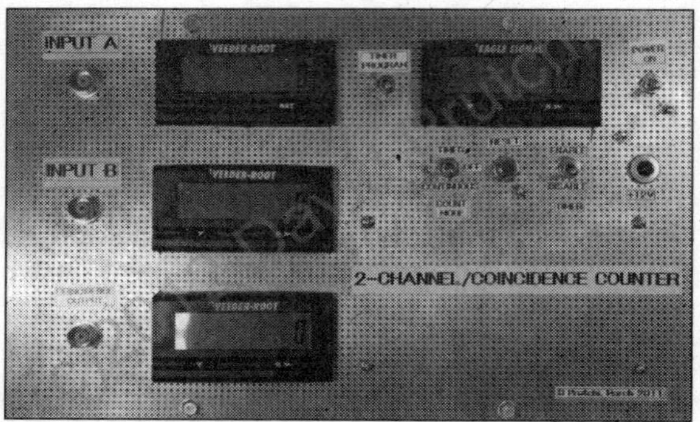

Coincidence circuit

Cold emission

It is an emission of electrons in strong st static electric fields.

Cold fusion

It is the nuclear fusion of atoms taking place in conditions near room temperature.

Colligative properties

These are physical properties of solutions that depend upon the number of solute particles present.

Collimator

It can refer to (i) an instrument for narrowing a beam or ray of particles or waves; (ii) a small fixed telescope used for setting the line of sight of a larger astronomical telescope.

Colloid

It is a heterogeneous mixture in which solute-like particles are in a suspended state.

Colorimeter

It is a light instrument used in colorimetric analysis for measuring the intensity and quantity of colour in relation to a specific set of standards.

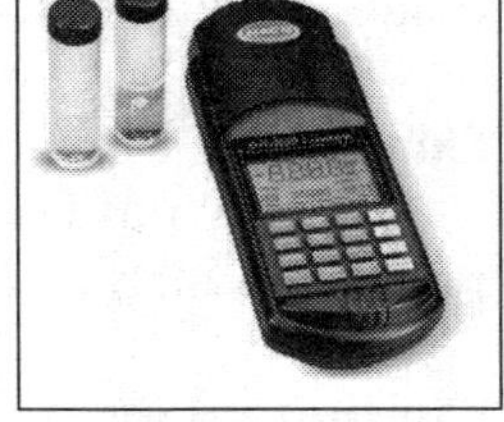

Colorimeter

Colour

It is the visual perceptual property in humans to the categories called red, green, blue and others.

Colour photography

It explains the processes which are produced chemically or using electronic sensors to record colour information during the photographic processing phase.

Colour television

It is a television that transmits images in colour, in contrast to black-and-white images.

Combustion

It is the swift chemical combination of a substance with oxygen with the generation of heat and light.

Comet

It is a small celestial body comprising a nucleus of ice and dust that moves around the sun in a highly elliptical orbit.

Communication satellite

It is an artificial satellite, which is an electronic retransmission vehicle, stationed in space in a fixed earth orbit for the purpose of telecommunications.

Commutator

It is a switch (device) for reversing the direction of flow of electric current.

Compass

It is a navigational instrument with a magnetized pointer, which is used mainly for finding directions.

Compound machine

It is machine consisting of two or more simple machines.

Compound machine

Compound microscope

It is a light microscope with multiple lenses which chiefly has two converging lens systems known as the objective and the eyepiece.

Compressed air

It is the air which has been reduced in volume and increased in pressure, and is used to power machinery, etc.

Compton effect

It is the interaction of photons, usually X rays, with

electrons in matter resulting in increased wavelength of X rays and kinetic energy of electrons.

Computer

It is an electronic programmable machine for storing and processing data and information, usually in binary form, and it provides output in a useful format.

Computer

Concave lens

It refers to a diverging lens, which is thinner in center than edges.

Concave mirror

It refers to a converging mirror, in which one with center of curvature on reflecting side of mirror.

Condensation

It is the liquefaction of vapour.

Conduction

It is the phenomenon by which heat or electricity is directly conveyed through a material without its movement.

Conduction band

It refers to the energies of charge carries in a solid such that the carriers are free to move.

Conductor

It is the material through which charged particles move or heat flows readily.

Configuration

It is the fixed arrangement of the atoms in a molecule.

Congelation

It is the process of passing, or causing to pass, from a fluid to a solid state, as by the abstraction of heat.

Conics

It is the branch of geometry which includes the study of curves, such as circles, ellipses, hyperbolas and parabolas, formed when a cone is cut by a plane.

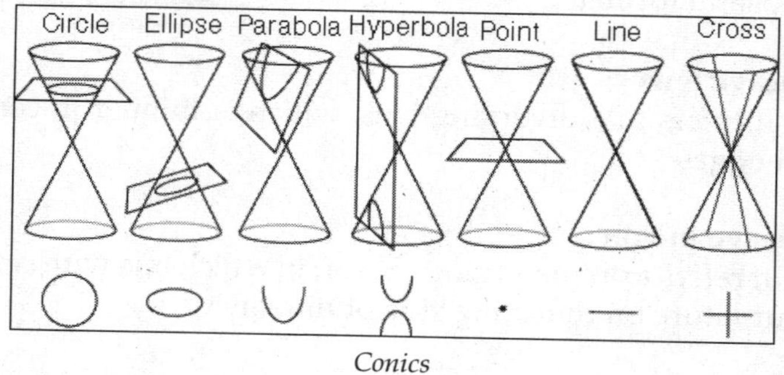

Conics

Conjunction

It is an apparent meeting of two planets or other celestial objects, appearing to be in the same place in the sky.

Conservation law

It states that there is no change in a particular measurable property of an isolated physical system when it evolves or is developing.

Conserved properties

It is the property that is the same before and after an interaction.

Consolute temperature

Also called the upper critical solution temperature, it is a temperature at which two partially miscible liquids become fully miscible as the temperature is increased.

Consonance

It is a situation when two or more sounds sound pleasant when heard together.

Constant acceleration

It is an acceleration that does not alter in time.

Constant velocity

It is a velocity that does not alter in time.

Constantan

This copper–nickel alloy with high electrical resistance and a low temperature coefficient is mainly used in electrical work, such as thermocouples, wires, etc.

Constantan

Constructive interference

It refers to the superposition of waves resulting in a combined wave with amplitude larger than the component waves.

Containment

It is a system made for resisting the accidental release of radioactive material from a reactor to an outside environment.

Continuous spectrum

It has all wave-lengths in a specified region of the electromagnetic spectrum.

Continuous wave

Another name for continuous waveform, it is an electromagnetic wave of constant amplitude and frequency.

Control rod

It is steel or aluminium rod of a neutron-absorbing

substance without fissioning itself and is used to control the output power of a nuclear reactor.

Control unit

It is a part of the central processing unit that works with arithmetic logic unit by fetching and decoding commands as well as retrieving and storing information.

Convection

It refers to the heat transfer by means of motion of fluid.

Conventional current

It is the motion of positive electrical current.

Converging lens

It is a lens that causes light rays to converge, and is usually a convex lens.

Converter

It is a device for changing the nature of an electric current or signal from AC to DC or vice-versa.

Convex lens

It is a lens that is thicker in the center than at edges.

Convex mirror

It is a diverging mirror, wherein the center of curvature is on the side opposite to the reflecting side of the mirror.

Convex mirror

Coolant

It is a fluid agent (liquid or gas) that is used to remove heat from one part to another or prevent its overheating.

Coordination number

It refers to the number of atoms or ions around a central atom in a crystal.

Copernican astronomy

Named after Nicholas Copernicus, it states that earth and other planets of the solar system revolve around the sun, and earth rotates daily on its axis, completing one rotation in 24 hours.

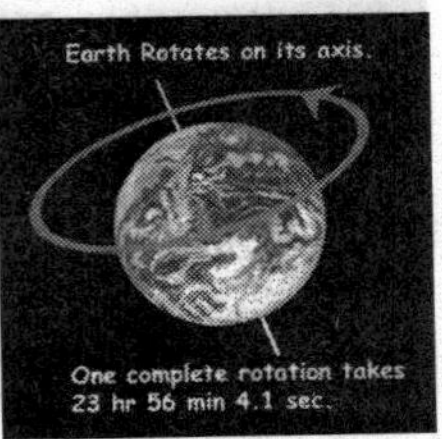

Copernican astronomy

Corona

Synonymous with aureole, it is the rarefied gaseous envelope of the sun and other stars, which can be seen as a halo only during a total solar eclipse.

Corrosion

It is the oxidation of metals in the presence of air and moisture.

Cosine

It refers to the ratio of the adjacent side to the hypotenuse.

Cosmic radiation

It is the penetrating ionizing radiation consisting of cosmic rays and high-energy particles coming from outside the solar system.

Cosmology

It is the metaphysical study of the origin and development of the universe.

Coulomb

It is a unit of electrical charge caused by flow of one ampere for one second.

Coulomb's law

It is a fundamental principle of electrostatics stating that like charges repel and opposite charges attract, with a force proportional to the product of the charges and inversely proportional to the square of the distance between them.

CPU

Known as the Central Processing Unit in the computer system, it is the main logic unit (a microprocessor chip) in the machine, which does most of the data processing.

CPU

Crack

It is a thin and usually jagged space opened in a formerly solid material.

Creep

It refers to the deformation of a plastic solid happening gradually under stress.

Crest of wave

It refers to the high point of wave motion.

Critical angle

It is the minimum angle of incidence that produces total internal reflection.

Critical pressure

It is the pressure of a gas or vapour in its critical state.

Critical reaction

It is a reaction in which one neutron from every fission event leads to another fission event, thus continuing the chain reaction.

Critical state

It is the state when the substance is at its critical point (at critical temperature, volume and pressure).

Critical temperature

It is the temperature of a gas in its critical state.

Crucible

This refractory container (ceramic or metal) is used for high temperature chemical reactions, so that the metals or other substances may be melted in it for laboratory processes.

Cryogenics

It is the science and study of the branch of physics dealing with the production and effects of very low temperatures.

Cryohydrate

It is a mechanical mixture of ice crystals and solid salt crystals in which the latter is precipitated at temperatures below 0°C.

Cryometer

It is a thermometer for measuring very low temperatures.

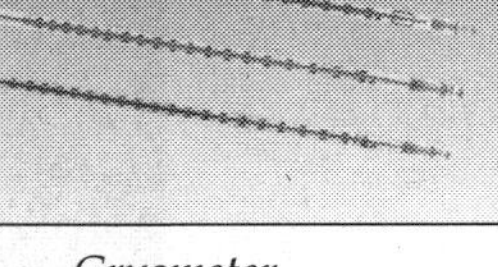

Cryometer

Cryostat

It is a thermostat for maintaining cold cryogenic temperatures.

Cryotron

It is a miniature switching element that operates using superconductivity, related to the principle that magnetic fields lead to the destruction of superconductivity.

Crystal

It is a homogeneous solid material, which has a natural geometrically regular form and is arranged in an orderly repeating pattern extending in all three spatial dimensions.

Crystal lattice

It is the structure of solid consisting of regular arrangement of atoms.

Crystallography

It is the branch of science dealing with the study of the structure, formation and properties of crystals.

Crystal microphone

It is a microphone in which sound waves vibrate a piezoelectric crystal which produces the electrical signal that is amplified as audio.

Crystal oscillator

It is an apparatus that generates electrical oscillations at a frequency based on the physical characteristics of a piezoelectric quartz crystal.

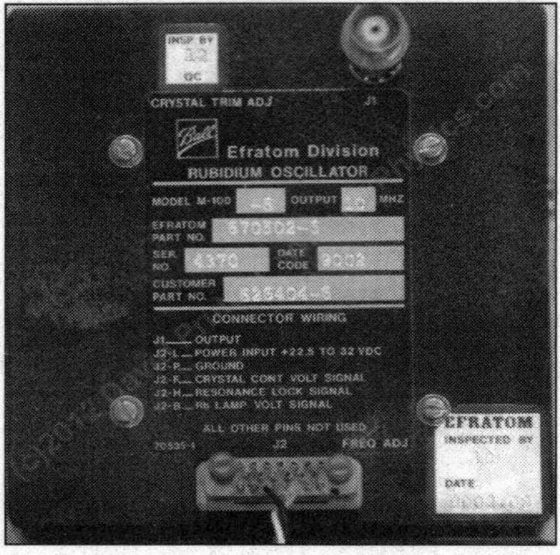

Crystal oscillator

Curie's law

It is a law stating that the magnetic susceptibility of a paramagnetic dipole is inversely proportional to the absolute temperature.

Curium [Cm]

Produced artificially by bombarding plutonium with helium nuclei, this synthetic radioactive, transuranic, metallic element, with its atomic number as 96, is used in space exploration.

Current [symbol: I]

Also called electric current, it is a phenomenon wherein electricity flows due to the ordered directional motion of electrically charged particles.

□

Dalton's atomic theory

Named after the English chemist, John Dalton, this modern atomic theory states that (i) elements are made of atoms (particles); (ii) atoms cannot be produced, subdivided, or destructed; (iii) atoms of different elements combine to form compounds.

Damping

It refers to any effect that reduces the amplitude of oscillations in an oscillatory system due to the energy being drained from the system to get over frictional or other forces.

Daniell cell

Invented by John Daniell, it is an electrochemical cell in which a reaction takes place between zinc metal and aqueous copper ions.

Daniell cell

Dark energy

It is a hypothetical kind of energy that permeates all of space, counteracts gravity and tends to accelerate the rate of expansion of the universe.

Dark galaxy

It is a hypothetical galaxy-sized object consisting of very few or no stars and is held together by dark matter.

Darmstadtium [Ds]

It is a synthetic, superheavy, radioactive, transuranic metallic element with its atomic number as 110.

Database

It refers to an organized and ordered collection of data for one or more purposes, usually in digital form.

Dating techniques

These are techniques of determining the age of rocks, palaeontological specimens, archaeological sites, etc.

Daughter nuclide

This nuclide is generated in a nuclear decay.

Day

It is a span of twenty-four hours as a unit of time corresponding to a rotation of the earth on its axis.

Death of a star

It refers to the end of a star's life, when it finally collapses.

Death of a star

De Broglie wavelength

It is the length of De Broglie wave of particle.

Debye

It is the unit used to denote dipole moments.

Debye-Huckel theory

This theory in physical chemistry explains the deviation

from ideality in solutions of electrolytes because of the electrical forces between ions.

Decay

It is a process concerning a radioactive substance which undergoes change to a different form by emitting radiation.

Decibel

It is a common measure of sound intensity that is one-tenth of a Bel on the logarithmic intensity scale.

Decoherence

Another name for dephasing, it is the process by which quantum systems interact with their environments without any interference between states of the system.

Degaussing

Named after Carl Friedrich Gauss, it is a mechanism of reducing or removing an unwanted magnetic field in a magnetic material such that its remnant magnetism is zero.

Degenerate gas

It is a super-compressed and very dense gas whose temperature does not depend on the pressure.

Degrees of freedom

This term conveys the dependence on parameters, and suggests the potentiality of counting the number of those parameters.

Dehydration

It is described as a state which involves the loss of water from the substance (or molecule).

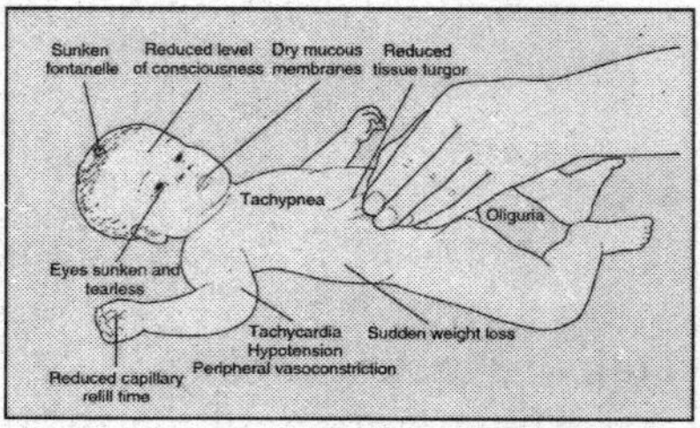

Dehydration

Deionised water

Produced through the use of ion exchange resins, it is the water consisting of only hydrogen, oxygen and hydroxyl ions.

Deliquescence

It is a phenomenon in which a hygroscopic substance takes in moisture from the atmosphere till it dissolves in the concentrated solution.

Demagnetisation

It is the process of removing magnetisation from a material.

Demodulation

It refers to the reception of a signal by extracting it from a modulated carrier wave.

Denature

It means to add non-fissionable material to fissionable material to make it unsuitable for use as an atomic bomb or weapon.

Densitometer

It is a device for measuring and determining optical or photographic density of a semi-transparent material or of a reflecting surface.

Densitometer

Density

It denotes the mass of a substance per unit of volume.

Dependent variable

It is a variable that responds to change in manipulated variable.

Depolarisation

It means a loss of polarity.

Derivative

It is a compound that arises from a parent compound by replacement of one atom with a group of atoms.

Derived units

It is a unit of quantity that consists of combination of fundamental units.

Desorption

It is the removal of an adsorbed substance from the surface of a solid adsorbent.

Destructive interference

It is the superposition of waves resulting in a combined wave with zero amplitude.

Deuterated compound

It describes a compound which has had some or all of its hydrogen replaced with the heavy isotope deuterium.

Deuterium [D]

It is an isotope of hydrogen whose atoms have both a proton and a neutron in the nucleus.

Deuterium oxide

Another name for heavy water, it is the water having a substantial proportion of deuterium atoms.

Dew

These tiny drops of water that form on cool surfaces at night are a result of the condensation of atmospheric vapour.

Dew

Dew point

It refers to the atmospheric temperature at which the water vapour in the air becomes saturated and then condensation occurs.

Diamagnetism

It is the weak repulsion by a magnetic field.

Diamond

Known as the hardest substance found in nature, this clear, colourless, crystalline form of pure carbon is used as a semi-conductor, gemstone, etc.

Diamond

Diastereoisomers

Also called diastereomers, these are stereoisomers that are not related as mirror images.

Dielectric heating

It describes the heating of an insulator by a high-frequency electric field due to the internal losses during the fast polarization reversal of molecules in the material.

Differential thermal analysis

Abbreviated as DTA, it is a method for observing the temperature, direction, and magnitude of thermally induced transitions in a substance.

Diffraction

It is the bending of waves around object in their path.

Diffraction grating

It is the material containing many parallel lines very closely spaced that generates a light spectrum by interference.

Diffuse reflection

It is the reflection of light into many directions by a rough object.

Diffusion

It is a process in which the substances intermingle by the natural movement of their particles (going from high to low concentration).

Digitron

Also called nixie tube, it is an electronic instrument which has a common anode and several cathodes in the form of characters, and it is used for displaying numerals or other information using glow discharge.

Dilatancy

It is a phenomenon in which some fluids become thicker under pressure.

Dilatometer

This scientific instrument is used for measuring volume changes (expansion or contraction) as a result of a physical or chemical process, such as heating, cooling, polymorphic changes, etc.

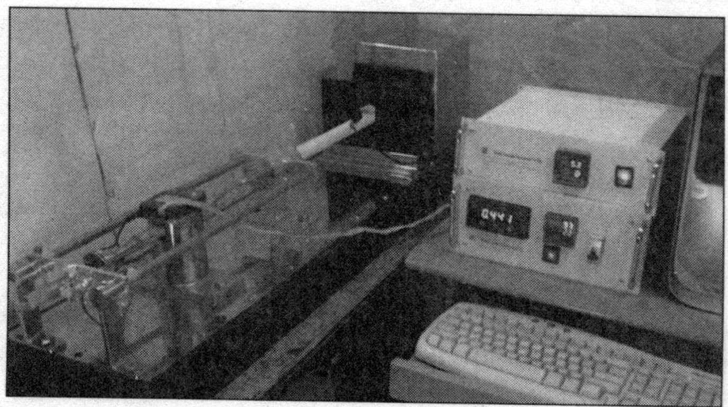

Dilatometer

Dilute

It is thinning the concentration of a solution by adding another solvent to it.

Dimensional analysis

It refers to checking a derived equation by making sure dimensions are the same on both sides.

Diode

It is an electrical device permitting only one way current flow.

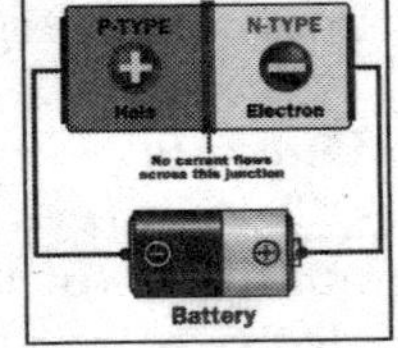

Diode

Direct current

Abbreviated as DC, it is an electric charge that flows in one direction continuously.

Disintegration

It is a phenomenon in which an atomic nucleus or other subatomic particle disintegrates and splits into smaller particles.

Disperse phase

Also called discontinuous phase, it is the solute-like species in a colloid.

Dispersion of light

It refers to the variation with wavelength of speed of light through matter resulting in separation of light into spectrum.

Displacement [symbol: s]

It is a vector quantity of scalar distance.

Dissonance

It describes two or more sounds that sound unpleasant when heard together.

Distance

It refers to a scalar quantity related to the separation between two points.

Diverging lens

It is a concave lens that causes light rays to spread apart or diverge.

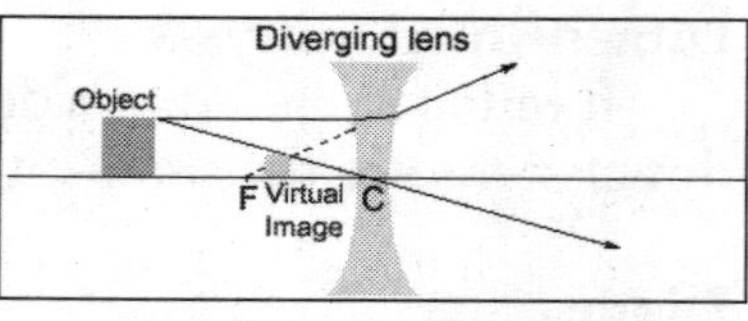

Diverging lens

Dopants

It refers to the small quantities of material added to semiconductor to increase electrical conduction.

Doppler shift

It is the change in wavelength due to relative motion of source and detector.

Dosimeter

It is a device used for measuring a dose of ionising radiation.

Doublet

It is the pair of two peaks or bands of about equal intensity appearing close together on a spectrogram.

Dry cell

These are ordinary batteries (voltaic cells) in which the electrolyte is in the form of a paste preventing it from flowing.

Dry ice

Sometimes called card ice, it is the frozen solid form of carbon dioxide, which is used chiefly as a refrigerant.

Dubnium [Db]

Produced by high-energy atomic collisions, it is an unstable, transuranic, synthetic, radioactive element with its atomic number as 105.

Ductility

It describes the quality or capability in a material of having its shape changed permanently by means of applied mechanical force.

DVD

Known as Digital Video Disc, it is a kind of compact disc which can store large amounts of data, such as high-resolution audio-visual information.

Dwarf planet

It is a celestial body similar to a small planet orbiting a star, but is not a satellite and is not large enough to qualify as a major planet.

Dwarf star

It is a star which is too small to be classified as a giant star or a supergiant star.

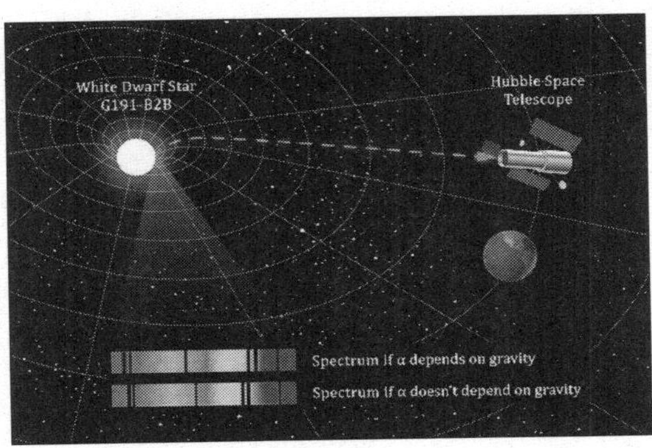

Dwarf star

Dynamics

It is the study of motion of particles acted on by forces.

Dynamo

It is an electrical generator, in which mechanical energy is transformed into electrical energy.

Dynamometer

It is a device for measuring the power output of an engine.

Dyne [symbol: dyn]

It is a unit of force in the c.g.s. system that is equal to the force which produces a velocity of one centimeter per second acting on one gram for one second.

□

E

Earth

This is the planet on which life is found. It is the third planet from the sun and acts as a big magnet with North and South poles as centres of attraction.

Earth's atmosphere

It is a layer of gases surrounding the Earth that is retained by its gravity. This layer of gases protects life by absorbing UV rays, keeping the planet's surface warm through heat retention, and reducing temperature extremes between day and night.

Echo

It is the repetition of a sound or series of sounds resulting from the reflection or reverberation of sound waves from a surface back to the hearer.

Eclipse

It is an astronomical occurrence when there is a temporary obscuring of the light from one celestial body by the passage of

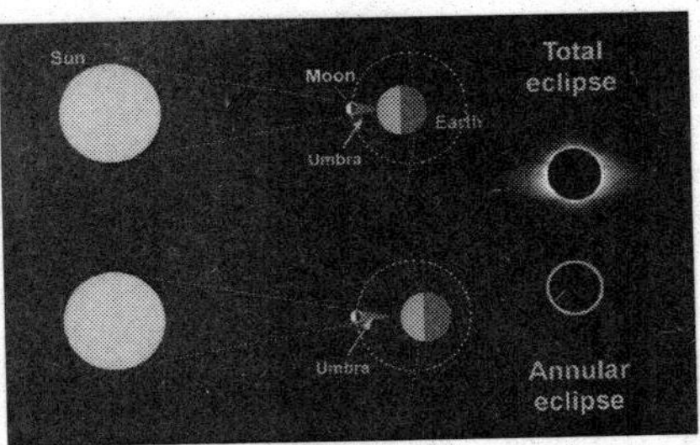

Eclipse

another between it and the viewer or between it and its source of illumination.

Effective current

It refers to the DC current that would generate the same heating effects.

Effective voltage

It refers to the DC potential difference that would generate the same heating effects.

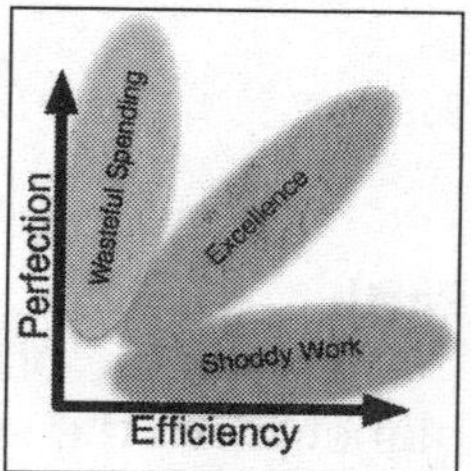

Efficiency

Efficiency

It is the ratio of output work to input work.

Effort force

It refers to the force extended on a machine.

Effusion

It is the process in which there is a flow of gas molecules through a small opening without collisions between molecules.

Einstein equation

Also known as mass-energy equivalence, $E = mc^2$, it is the principle that a measured quantity of mass is equal to a measured quantity of energy.

Einsteinium [symbol: Es]

Created by bombarding plutonium with neutrons, it is a radioactive, transuranic, synthetic element of the actinide series, with its atomic number as 99.

Ekpyrotic universe

Also called the ekpyrotic scenario, it is a cosmological model of the origin and shape of the universe, which states that our current universe came into being from a collision of two three-dimensional worlds in space with an extra spatial dimension.

Elastic collision

It is an interaction between two objects in which the total energy is the same before and after the interaction.

Elasticity

It is the ability of object to original shape after there is a removal of deforming forces.

Electrical charge pump

It is a device, often a battery or generator, which increases the potential of electrical charge.

Electrical circuit

It describes a continuous path through which electrical charges can flow.

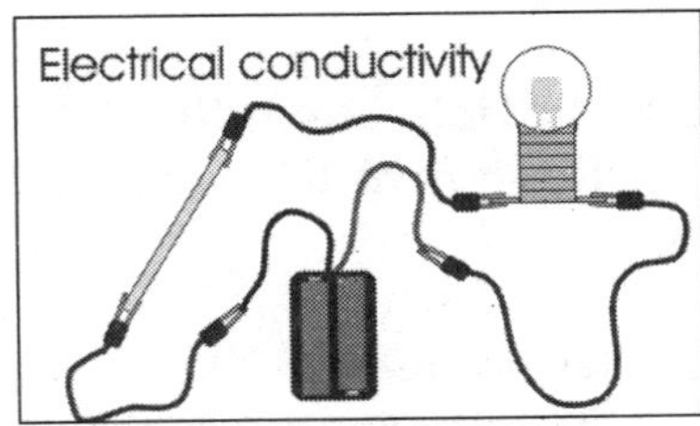

Electrical conductivity

Electrical conductivity

It is the ability to conduct electricity.

Electrical current

It refers to the flow of charged particles.

Electrical field

It is the property of space around a charged object that causes forces on other charged objects.

Electric arc

Synonymous with arc discharge, it is the electrical conduction through a gas in an applied electric field, which generates a flowing plasma discharge.

Electric bell

This bell consists of an electromagnet, an armature with a hammer and a cup, all of which are activated by the magnetic effect of an electric current.

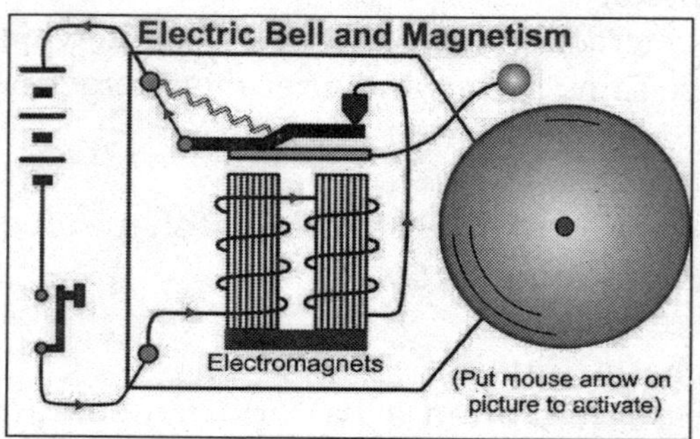

Electric bell

Electric field lines

It describes the lines representing the direction of electric field.

Electric field strength

It refers to the ratio of force exerted by field on a tiny test.

Electric generator

It is a device converting mechanical energy into electrical energy.

Electric lighting

It explains illumination or lighting generated through the means of electricity.

Electric motor

It is a motor (device) that converts electricity to mechanical work through the interaction of magnetic fields and current-carrying conductors, which are often used in accessories such as power windows or power seats, etc.

Electric potential [symbol: V]

It is the ratio of electric potential energy to charge.

Electric potential difference

It refers to the difference in electric potential between the two points.

Electric potential energy

It is the energy of a charged body in an electrical field.

Electrocardiogram

Abbreviated as ECG, it is a test in which a graphical recording of the cardiac cycle (heart's health) is generated by an electrocardiograph.

Electrochemical cell

This device consists of an anode and a cathode in metallic contact and immersed in an electrolyte, which either draws electrical energy from reactions or produces reactions through electrical energy.

Electrochemical equivalent

It is the weight of a substance that is accumulated at an electrode when one coulomb of electricity charge is passed.

Electrochemistry

It is the study of chemical action generated by electrical current and the creation of electricity by chemical reactions.

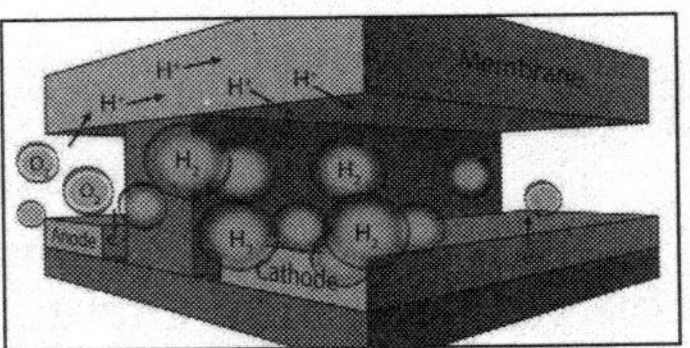

Electrochemistry

Electrode

It is a conductor through which electricity comes in or goes out of a substance.

Electrodeposition

It is the deposition of a substance (metal or rubber) on

an electrode by the action of electricity or when electricity is passed through a solution.

Electrode potential

It is the potential difference between the charge on an electrode and in the solution.

Electrodialysis

It is a method in which electrical current is applied to permeable membranes for the removal of charged particles from water.

Electrodynamics

It is the branch of mechanical phenomena dealing with moving electric charges and their interaction of electric currents with magnetic fields or other currents.

Electrolysis

This phenomenon that takes place in electrolytic cells is a chemical decomposition reaction generated by passing electric current through a solution having ions.

Electrolyte

It is a substance whose aqueous solutions containing positive or negative ions conduct electricity.

Electrolytic cell

It is a cell in which chemical reactions take place when an outside source of electrical energy is applied.

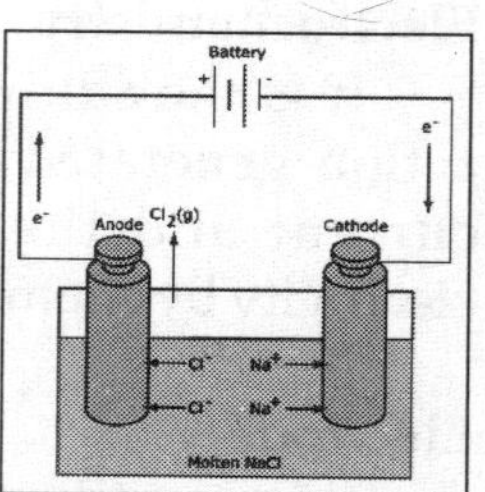

Electrolytic cell

Electrolytic corrosion

Also called electrochemical corrosion, it is a corrosion resulting from the contact of two different metals in the presence of a conducting fluid (electrolyte).

Electrolytic gas

Produced by the electrolysis of water, it is a mixture of two parts of hydrogen and one part of oxygen by volume.

Electrolytic refining

It is the phenomenon of the purification of metal ingots which are in suspension as anodes in an electrolytic bath, alternated with refined sheets of the same metal as cathodes.

Electromagnet

It is an instrument that uses an electric current to produce a concentrated magnetic field.

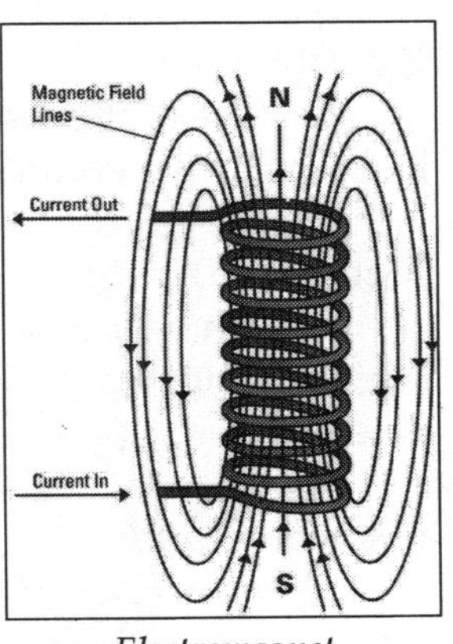

Electromagnet

Electromagnetic force

It is one of fundamental forces due to electric charges, which include both static and moving.

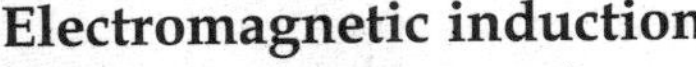

Electromagnetic induction

It is the generation of electric field or current due to change in magnetic flux.

Electromagnetic radiation

It is the wave-like form of energy that is transmitted by means of electric and magnetic fields, which vary at the same time.

Electromagnetic waves

It is a wave containing oscillating electric and magnetic fields that move at speed of light through space.

Electrometer

It is an electrical instrument for measuring electric charge or electrical potential difference without taking in any current from the circuit.

Electromotive force

Commonly known as emf, it is the difference in potential that tends to develop an electric current (electrons, ions).

Electromotive series

Another name for activity series, it is the relative order of elements or ions in order of their electrode potentials ascertained under specified circumstances.

Electron

It is one of the three atomic particles of small mass, which has a negative charge (–1) found in every atom.

Electron affinity

It is the amount of energy absorbed in the process in which an electron is added to a neutral gaseous atom to form a negative ion (–1).

Electron cloud

It is an area of high probability of finding an electron around an atom.

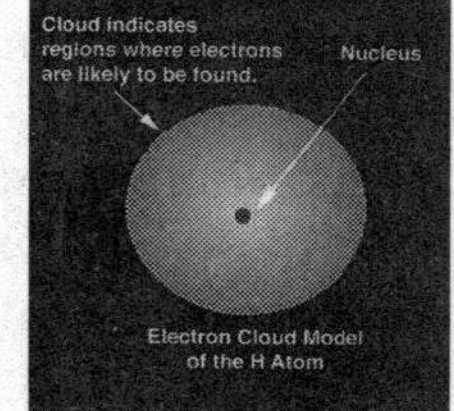

Electron cloud

Electron diffraction

It is the effect on electrons due to wave-like interference of electrons with matter.

Electron gas model

It is the description of electric current flow through conductors.

Electron gun

It is a cathode/anode device for producing a narrow stream of electrons from a heated cathode in a cathode-ray tube or electron microscope.

Electronics

It is the branch of physics and technology concerned with the behaviour, movement and effects of electrons and with the use of electronic devices and the design of circuits using transistors, microchips, etc.

Electron lens

It is an electronic equipment for focusing a beam of electrons, using electric or magnetic fields.

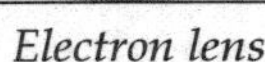

Electron lens

Electron microscope

It is a microscope with high magnification and resolving power, by the means of electron beams instead of light and using electron lenses to illuminate the object.

Electronegativity

It is a measure of the relative tendency of an atom to attract electrons to itself when chemically combined with another atom.

Electrophoresis

Synonymous with cataphoresis, it is a method for separating charged particles in a colloid when in an electric field.

Electrophoretic effect

This trend of the applied potential to move the ionic atmosphere itself slows down the movement of ions within a solution.

Electrophorus

It is a simple electrostatic generator for repeatedly generating static electricity by induction.

Electroplating

It is the process of plating a metal onto a surface with the use of electrical current.

Electropositive

It pertains to elements which lose electrons and form positive ions in chemical reactions.

Electroscope

It is an equipment to detect electric charges.

Electrostatic generator

It is an electrical device used to build up a static electric charge to an extreme potential for producing electricity.

Electrostatic generator

Electrostatic precipitation

In this process, there is a removal of suspended dust particles from an air stream by attraction and adhesion of ionised particles to an electrode.

Electrostatics

It is the study of properties and results of electric charges at rest.

Electroweak force

It is the unification of electromagnetic and weak forces.

Electrum

It is a natural or artificial alloy of gold and silver with minute amounts of copper and other metals, which is used mainly in jewellery-making.

Element

A chemical element is a substance made of atoms which cannot be broken down into simpler forms. There are 92 elements which are naturally found.

Elementary charge

It is the magnitude of the charge of an electron.

Elinvar

It is a nickel-steel alloy consisting of other additions such as chromium, manganese, titanium, etc. with a modulus of elasticity which does not change much over the range of temperatures.

Ellipse

It is a regular oval shape as a result of the intersection of a circular cone and a plane cutting completely through it.

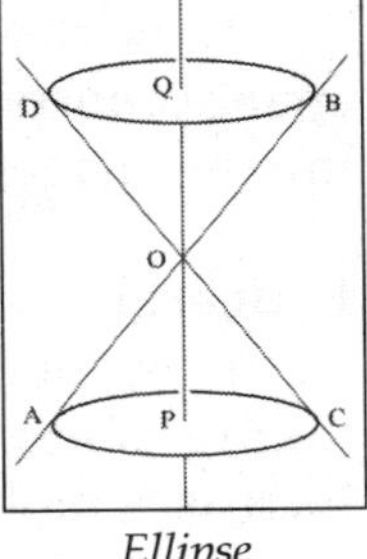

Ellipse

Eluent

It is the solvent used in the process of elution for separating materials.

Elution

It is a method of separating materials that are absorbed using a solvent.

Elutriation

Another name for air classification, it is a process for separating lighter particles from heavier ones with the use of a vertically-directed stream of air or liquids.

Emission spectrum

It is a spectrum related to emission of electromagnetic radiation by atoms due to electronic transitions from higher to ground energy levels.

Empirical formula

It is the formula of a substance or compound, where relative numbers of atoms of each element are shown.

Emulsion

It is the colloidal suspension in which both phases are liquids.

Enantiomer

It is one of the two mirror-image forms of an optically active molecule.

Enantiomorphism

It is the relationship demonstrated by a pair of enantiomorphs (compounds that are non-superimposable mirror images of each other).

Endoergic

It is concerning a nuclear reaction or transformation taking place with absorption of energy which usually increases molecular potential energy.

Endothermic

It refers to chemical reactions that absorb heat energy from its surroundings.

Energy

It is the non-material property to do work or transfer heat, in effect causing changes in matter.

Energy level

It is the amount of energy an electron in an atom may have.

Engine

It is a machine with moving parts (motor) that converts power or thermal energy into motion or mechanical work.

Engine

Enrichment

It refers to the physical process of increasing the proportion of U-235 to U-238.

Enthalpy [symbol: H]

It is the heat content of a specific amount of substance.

Entropy [symbol: S]

It is a thermodynamic property that is a measure of the degree of disorder of a system.

Epicentre

It is that point on the earth's crust, which is directly above the focus of an earthquake, from where it originated.

Epidiascope

Also called episcope, it is an optical projector that provides images of both opaque and transparent objects by shining a bright lamp onto the object from above.

Equation of state

It describes the behaviour of matter in a given state.

Equator

This imaginary line that is around the earth is the intersection of a sphere's surface with the plane perpendicular to the sphere's axis of rotation and comprising the sphere's centre of mass.

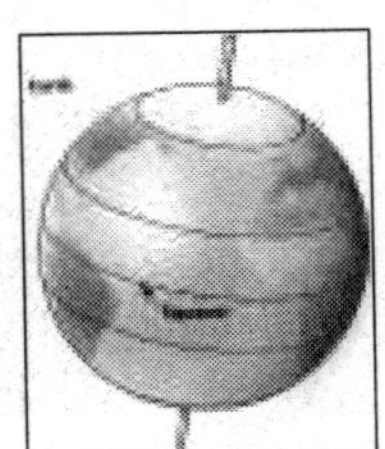

Equator

Equilibrant force

It refers to the force that is needed to bring an object into transitional equilibrium.

Equilibrium

It is a state of dynamic balance in which no changes take place and the rates of forward and reverse reactions are equal.

Equinox

This astronomical phenomenon takes place twice during the year, when the sun crosses the plane of the earth's equator, and the day and night are of equal length.

Equivalent resistance

It is the single resistance that could replace several resistors.

Ergonomics

It is the branch of engineering science in which biological science is used to study people's efficiency in their working environment.

Ether

Another name for ethyl ether, it is an aromatic, flammable, colourless, volatile liquid used as a solvent and intermediate.

Eudiometer

This laboratory device is used for measuring volume changes in chemical reactions between gases, and consists of a graduated glass tube in which mixtures of gases can be made to react by an electric spark.

Eudiometer

Eutectic mixture

Also called eutectic system, it is a mixture of substances or chemical compounds which have a melting point lower than that of any of its constituents.

Evaporation

It is the conversion of a liquid to the gaseous state (vapour).

Exciplex

It refers to any complex of two different atoms, existing in an excited state, which is dissociated in the ground state.

Excitation

It is the process in which an atom or other particle is raised to a higher energy state when energy is supplied.

Excited state

It is the energy level of atom higher than ground state.

Exoergic

It relates to a process or nuclear reaction occurring with evolution or releasing of energy, but also in the form of light, electricity or sound.

Exosphere

It is the outermost region or layer of a planet's atmosphere.

Exothermic

It describes chemical reactions which release heat energy.

Exotic atom

It is a normal atom in which one or more sub-atomic particles have been replaced by other particles of the same charge.

Extensometer

It is a device for measuring the deformation of an object under stress.

External forces

It refers to the forces exerted from outside a system.

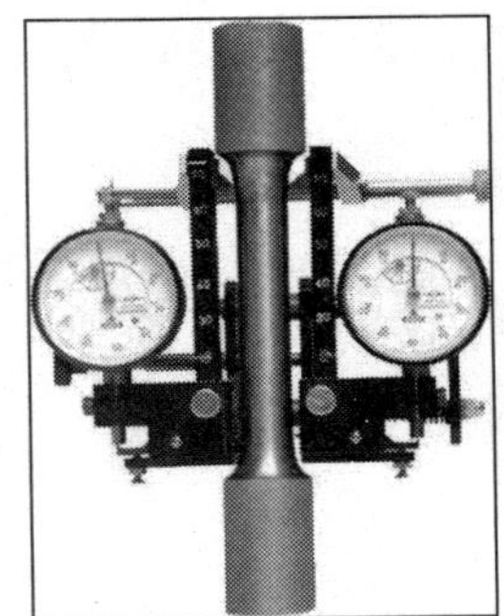

Extensometer

Extraction

It is the technique of deriving a component from a mixture by chemical means.

Extrapolate

It is an estimation of the value of a result outside the range of a series of known values.

Extrasolar planet

Another name for exoplanet, it is any planet that orbits stars outside the solar system.

Extrasolar planet

Extrinsic semiconductor

It is a semiconductor in which conduction is mainly the outcome of added impurities.

Eye

It refers to each of a pair of globular organs in the head that detect light, and convert it to electro-chemical impulses in neurons, which makes people and vertebrate animals see their surroundings.

□

F

Facet

It refers to the flat faces on geometric shapes reflecting the symmetry of the crystal structure.

Factor-label method

Another name for dimensional analysis, it is the sequential application of conversion factors expressed as fractions.

Fahrenheit scale

On this temperature scale, the freezing point of water is 32°F and the boiling point is 212°F.

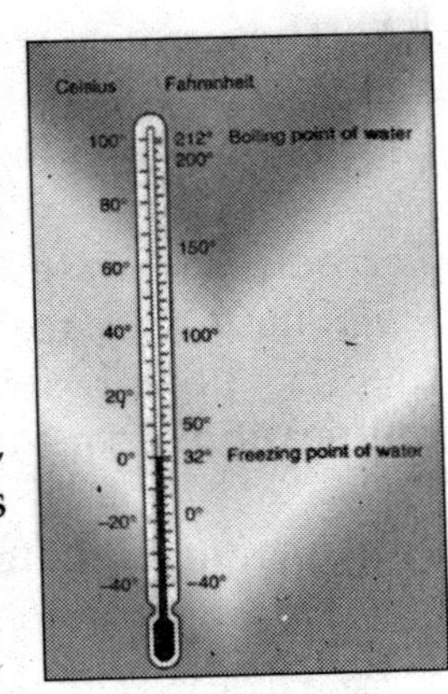

Fahrenheit scale

Fall-out

It is the residual radiation hazard, usually the radioactive dust, which falls out from a nuclear explosion.

Farad [symbol: F]

It is the unit of electrical capacitance, which is defined as one coulomb per volt.

Fast-ion conductor

Also known as superionic conductors, these are

materials that act as solid state ion conductors which are used mainly in solid oxide fuel cells.

Fermion

It is a subatomic particle with half-integral spin and obeys the Fermi and Dirac statistics.

Fermium [Fm]

Derived artificially by bombarding plutonium with neutrons, it is a radioactive, synthetic, transuranic metallic element of the actinide series, with its atomic number as 100.

Ferrite

This unstable, magnetic, ceramic compound with iron (III) oxide (Fe_2O_3) is used in making antennas, transformers, etc.

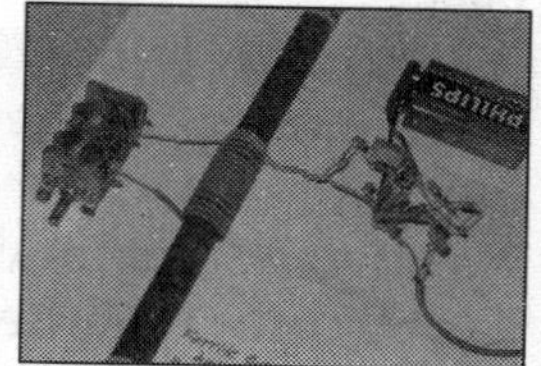

Ferrite

Ferroalloys

These are several alloys of iron with one or more other metals, such as manganese or silicon, which is used in steel production.

Ferroelectric materials

These are substances with the property of permanent electric polarization that varies in strength with the application of an external electric field.

Ferromagnetic materials

These are materials in which large internal magnetic fields are generated by cooperative action of electrons.

Ferromagnetism

It is the ability of a substance to become permanently magnetised in a magnetic field.

Fertiliser

This is a substance used to increase soil's fertility and improve plant growth.

Field coil

It is the magnetic field component of an alternator, generator, dynamo, etc. that generates the magneto motive force to set up the flux in an electric machine.

Film badge

It is a patch of photographic film worn to monitor accumulated ionising radiation.

Filter

It is a porous apparatus for eliminating impurities or particles from a liquid or gas.

Filter pump

Also called an aspirator, it is a device that generates vacuum using the Venturi effect to quicken the process of filtering.

Filter pump

Filtration

It is the process of filtering in which there is a separation of solids from fluids.

First harmonic

It is the fundamental frequency in music.

First law of thermodynamics

This law states that the change in internal or thermal energy is equal to heat added and work done on system.

Fissile material

It refers to any material in which neutrons are capable of sustaining a chain reaction of nuclear fission.

Fixed point

Also called defining point, it is a well-defined reproducible temperature that can be used as a standard.

Fixed stars

It refers to the celestial objects that appear to be motionless in relation to the other stars of the night sky because of their great distance from Earth.

Flame

It is a hot glowing body of ignited gas that is generated by combustion.

Flash memory

It is the memory that retains data when the power supply is not present.

Flash photolysis

It is a method of examining fast photochemical reactions in gases.

Flash point

It is the lowest temperature at which the vapour above liquid produces an inflammable mixture with air.

Flip-flop

It is an electronic circuit that is capable of assuming either of two stable states.

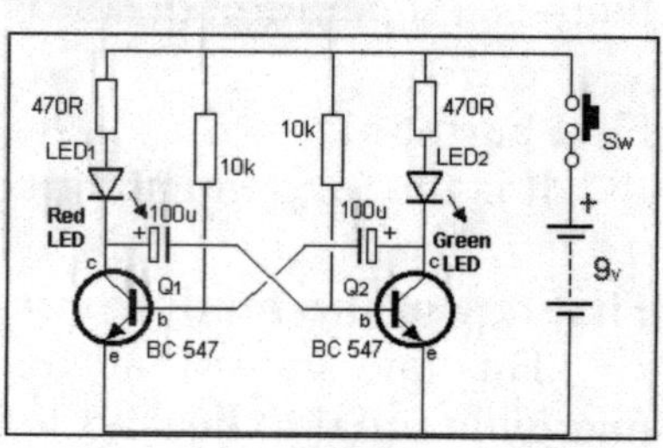

Flip-flop

Fluid

It describes a material that flows, including liquids, gases and plasmas.

Fluidics

Another name for fluidic logic, it is the study and

method of using small interacting flows and fluid jets for functions generally performed with electronics.

Fluidization

It is a phenomenon in which a granular material is transformed from a solid-like state to a fluid-like state.

Fluid mechanics

It is the branch of mechanics concerned with the properties of fluids in different conditions and with their reaction to forces acting upon them, which are based on physical analysis and experimental verification.

Fluorescence

It is the taking in of high energy radiation by a substance and resultant emission of visible light.

Flux

It is a substance added to a solid to lower its melting point, and is used mainly in soldering metals.

Fluxmeter

It is an instrument for measuring magnetic flux by the current it produces in a coil.

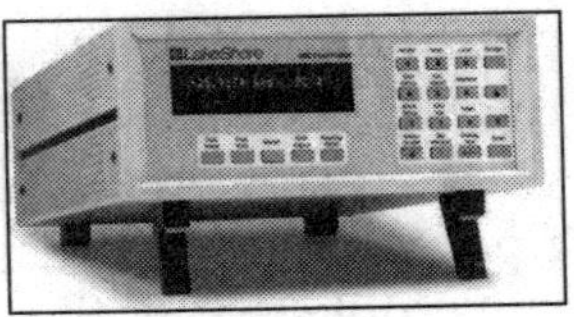

Fluxmeter

Foam

It is a mass of small bubbles dispersed in a liquid.

Focal length

It is the distance from the focal point to the center of a lens or vertex of a mirror.

Focal point

It is the location at which rays parallel to the optical axis of an ideal mirror or lens converge to a point.

Forbidden gap

It refers to the energy values that electrons in a semiconductor or insulator may not possess.

Forbidden mechanism

Also called forbidden line, it is a spectral line emitted by atoms undergoing nominally forbidden energy transitions.

Force [symbol: P]

It describes an agent that results in accelerating or deforming an object.

Force constant

It refers to the force controlling the relative displacement of the cell nucleus in a molecule.

Fossil fuels

Obtained from the decomposition of organic materials under geological conditions, these substances (coal, petroleum, natural gas) are carbon or hydrocarbon fuels.

Fossil fuels

f.p.s. units

Replaced by SI units, it is an imperial system of units based on the foot, pound, and second as the units of length, mass, and time.

Frame of reference

It is a coordinate system used to define motion.

Francium [Fr]

Found as disintegration product of actinium, it is a radioactive member of the alkali metal group, with its atomic number as 87.

Fraunhofer lines

It refers to the absorption lines in the sun's spectrum due to gases in the solar atmosphere.

Free-electron laser

Abbreviated as FEL, it is a laser which is similar to other lasers, but which makes use of some very different operating principles for forming and emitting the beam.

Free electron model

It refers to a model for the behaviour of valence electrons in a crystal structure of a metallic solid.

Free energy

It is the thermodynamic quantity equivalent to the amount of work that can be extracted from a physical system.

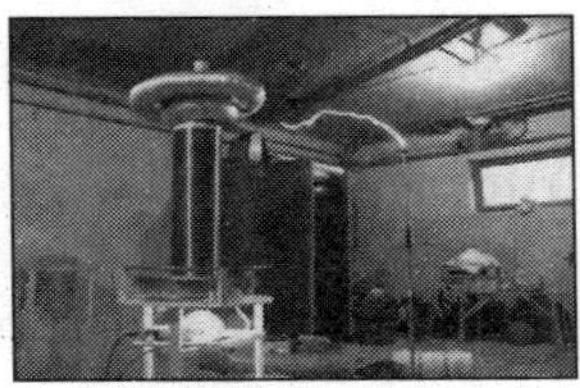

Free energy

Free fall

It is an ideal falling motion of a body where gravitational field is the dominant force acting upon it.

Free space

It is a concept of electromagnetic theory defined as the vacuum of free space.

Freeze drying

It is a technique of drying food or blood plasma or pharmaceuticals or tissue without destructing their physical structure.

Freezing mixture

It is a mixture of substances to get a temperature below 0°C.

Frequency [symbol: f or v]

It refers to the number of occurrences per unit time.

Friction

It is the force opposing relative motion of two objects, which are in contact.

Froth floatation

It is a method for separating hydrophobic substances from hydrophilic.

Fuel

It is a combustible substance such as coal, gas, or oil that is burned to produce heat or power or energy.

Fuel cell

It is a voltaic cell which converts the chemical energy of a fuel directly into electrical energy.

Fundamental particles

It refers to those particles (quarks and leptons) of which all materials are made.

Fundamental tone

It is the lowest frequency sound produced by a musical instrument.

Fundamental units

It is a set of units on which a measurement system is based, such as meter, second, kilogram, ampere, etc.

Fuse

It refers to the metal safety device in an electric circuit that melts to stop current flow when current is too much.

Fuse

Fusible alloys

It is any metal alloy or solder that can easily be fused at low temperatures.

Fusion

It can refer to (i) melting which is the phenomenon of heating a solid substance until it becomes liquid; (ii) a combination of two nuclei into one with release of energy.

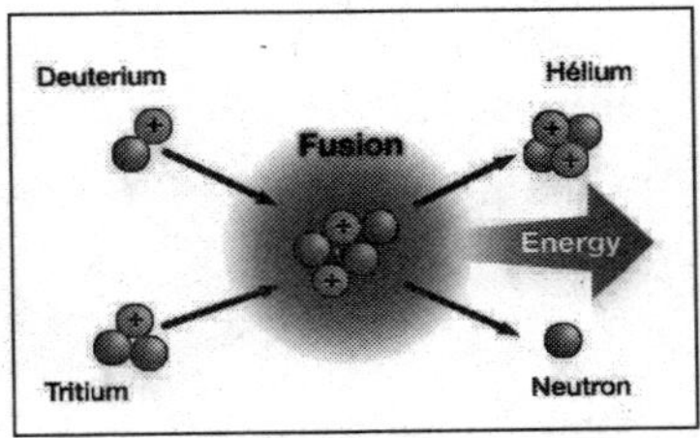

Fusion

Fusion reactor

It is a nuclear reactor in which a controlled thermonuclear fusion occurs to generate energy.

Fuzzy logic

It is a form of multi-valued mathematical logic derived from fuzzy set theory in which truth can assume a continuum of values between 0 and 1.

□

Galaxy

It is a massive collection of star systems, consisting of gas and dust, measuring many light years across, which is bound together by gravitational attraction.

Galaxy cluster

Also known as galaxy group, it forms the densest portion of the large scale structure of the universe. Simply, it is an assemblage of galaxies drawn to each other by gravitational attraction.

Galilean telescope

It is a kind of refracting telescope, having a biconvex objective and biconcave eyepiece, and has become outdated in the astronomical field.

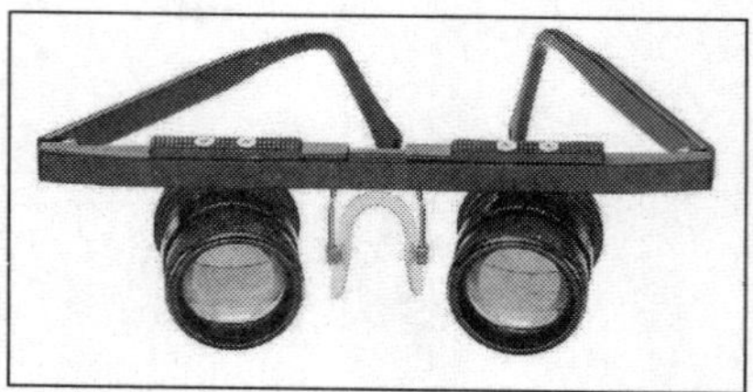

Galilean telescope

Galvanized iron

It is made by coating iron with zinc to prevent it from corroding.

Galvanising

It is defined as an application of a thin layer of zinc on

a ferrous material to avoid the surface under it from corroding.

Galvanometer

It is an instrument which is used for measuring very small currents.

Gamma camera

Also called Anger camera, it is an instrument used in nuclear medicine for imaging radioactive materials, such as gamma radiation.

Gamma camera

Gamma decay

It is a phenomenon during which a nucleus emits a gamma ray.

Gamma particle

It refers to a high energy photon emitted by a radioactive nucleus.

Gamma radiation

It is an electromagnetic radiation with high-energy, short wavelength emitted from an atom's nucleus.

Gas

It is defined as the state of matter that expands to fill a container.

Gas chromatography

This chromatography is used for segregating and examining gases' mixtures.

Gas laws

It refers to the physical laws that give a description of the properties of gases, predicting the behaviour of these gases when experiencing changes in pressure, temperature and volume.

Gas thermometer

It describes a type of thermometer, which makes use of the thermal properties of gas, as it measures temperature by alterations in the pressure of a gas kept at constant volume.

Gas turbine

It defines a kind of turbine driven by internal combustion through the expansion of hot gases produced by the chemical energy of a burning liquid fuel.

Gas turbine

Gaussmeter

Synonymous with magnetometer, it is a scientific instrument used to measure and compare the strengths and directions of the magnetic fields.

Geiger counter

It is a counter tube used for detecting and measuring ionising radiations.

Geiger-Mueller tube

It is an instrument used for detecting radiation by making use of its quality to ionise matter.

Gel

It is the colloidal suspension of a solid dispersed in a liquid.

General theory of relativity

It refers to an explanation of gravity and accelerated motion which was originally invented by Einstein.

Generator

It can refer to a dynamo, engine, or a machine that by the use of electromagnetic induction converts mechanical energy into electricity.

Generator

Geocentric universe

Also known as the Ptolemaic model of the universe, it describes a model of the universe that positions earth in the center with other objects or planets orbiting around it.

Geochemistry

It is defined as the study of earth's chemical composition or crust.

Geodesy

This scientific discipline, which is a branch of geology, deals with the measurement and shape of the earth, and the determination of the exact position of geographical points in a three-dimensional time-varying space.

Geodynamics

It refers to the branch of mechanics which is related to the forces inside the earth and their connection to the motion and equilibrium of the solid earth.

Geomagnetism

It refers to the branch of geology dealing with earth's magnetic fields and properties.

Geometric mean

It can be defined as a measure of the central or average tendency of a data set that avoids extreme values or positions.

Geophysics

It is that branch of geology that is concerned with

physical principles to study properties of the earth and its surrounding atmosphere.

Geothermal energy

Derived by deep-drilling in suitable geological areas, it is the energy or power extracted from heat stored in earth's interior.

German silver

It is a white-coloured alloy which consists of nickel, zinc and copper.

Giant star

It can be described as a very shiny star with a large radius and low density.

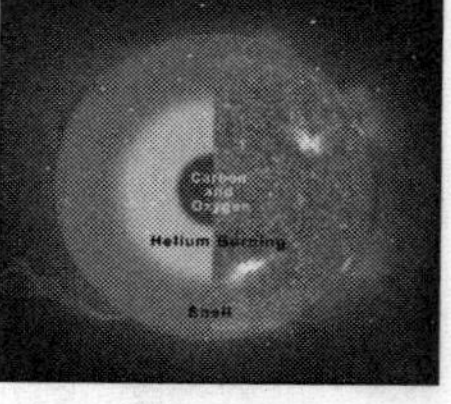

Giant star

Getter

It is a reactive substance used for the removal of residual gas from a vacuum system.

Glass

Prepared by mixing sand with soda, lime, and sometimes other components and cooling quickly, this non-crystalline material is typically hard, brittle, and often optically transparent or translucent. It is mainly used in making windows, drinking containers, and other useful things.

Glass electrode

Made of a doped glass membrane, it is a type of ion-selective electrode (half-cell).

Glass fibres

Another name for optical fibre, it is an extremely thin fibre or glass thread, which operates as a waveguide for light.

It is typically made of glass, and is used loosely and also in bundled form for reinforcement, tissue and textiles.

Glass transition

Also called vitrification, this dynamic process describes the transition of states with the transformation of a glass-forming liquid into a glass, which takes place after it quickly cools down.

Glove box

It refers to a closed model or workspace which has gloved openings allowing one to manipulate materials inside the enclosed chamber. The glove boxes are mainly useful when one desires a separate and controlled atmosphere.

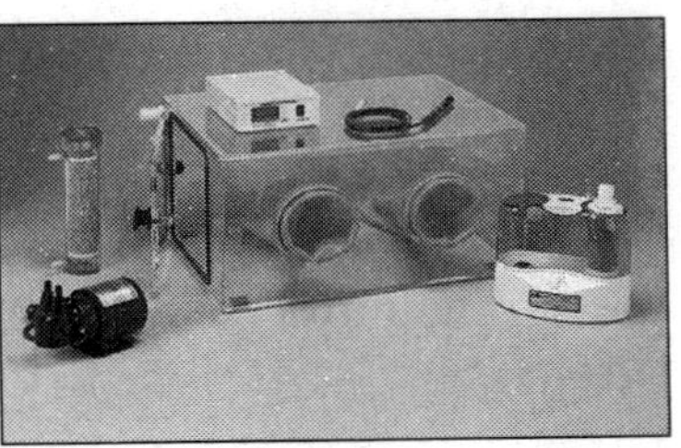

Glove box

Glow discharge

It can be defined as a kind of softly bright discharge or emission from electrical conduction in gases at low pressure.

Gluon

It is an elementary particle which carries strong nuclear force, and is assumed to bind quarks together.

Golay cell

Also called Golay detector, it is a kind of device that is mainly used as an opto-acoustic detector in infrared spectroscopy.

Gopher

It refers to a text-based menu system for browsing internet information, which is displayed through various menus.

Governor

It is a device that can regulate and maintain a stable speed in a machine by controlling the fuel supply.

Graham's law

This law states that the rates of effusion of gases are inversely proportional to the square roots of their densities.

Gram [symbol: g]

It is a metric unit of mass equal to one-thousandth of a kilogram.

Grand unified theories

It deals with the theories being generated that combine the stronger and electroweak forces into one force.

Graph

It is a diagram displaying the relation between certain variable quantities, which is measured along one of a set of axes at right angles.

Graphene

It refers to a monoatomic graphite sheet in which includes bonded carbon atoms, which are tightly arranged in a honeycomb crystal lattice.

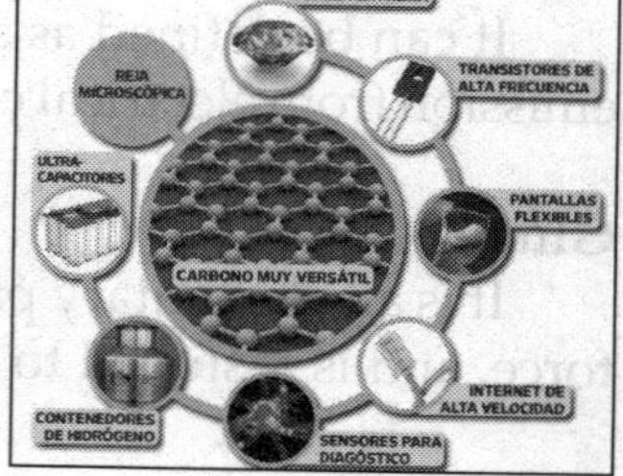

Graphene

Gravitational field

It can be defined as the space generated by the gravitational force and presence of mass.

Gravitational force

It can be described as (i) the force of attraction between all masses in the universe; (ii) the attraction between two objects due to their mass.

Gravitational mass

It refers to the mass of a body as ascertained by its gravitational force for other bodies.

Gravitational potential energy

It is the object's change of energy when moved within a gravitational field.

Graviton

It is a hypothetical particle or a gauge boson that carries the gravitational force.

Gravity

It is defined as the force of attraction that draws a body towards the center of the earth, or which exists between all the masses present in the universe.

Gray [symbol: Gy]

It is the SI unit of the absorbed dose of ionising radiation, which equals to one joule per kilogram.

Greenhouse effect

It is a process in which the solar radiation going out of the planet's surface is absorbed by the greenhouse gases, which results in warming of the planet.

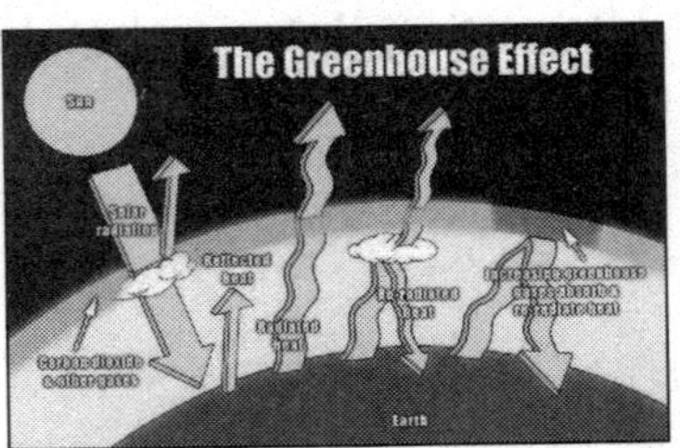

Greenhouse effect

Grey body

It is an idealized object that absorbs and emits electromagnetic radiation in constant proportion to the corresponding black-body radiation falling on it.

Ground state

It can be described as the lowest energy state of an atom, or a molecule.

Grounding

It is a phenomenon in which a charged object to the earth is connected for the removal of an object's unbalanced charge.

Gun metal

It refers to a kind of bronze, which is an alloy of copper, tin, and zinc, and was used mainly for manufacturing guns.

Gyrocompass

It can be defined as a nonmagnetic compass that makes use of a gyroscope whose axis is parallel to the earth's axis of rotation, and is, therefore, not dependent on magnetism.

Gyrocompass

Gyroscope

It is an instrument, which includes a wheel or a disk, and is used for determining or providing stability, which are based on the principles of conservation of angular momentum. These can, thus, be used in navigation systems, automatic pilots, and stabilizers to maintain a reference direction.

□

H

Hadron

It denotes any subatomic particle (e.g., baryons and mesons) having a strong force, which can take part in the strong interaction with other particles.

Half cell

Commonly known as an electrode, it is the structure in a voltaic cell in which the oxidation or reduction half-reaction takes place.

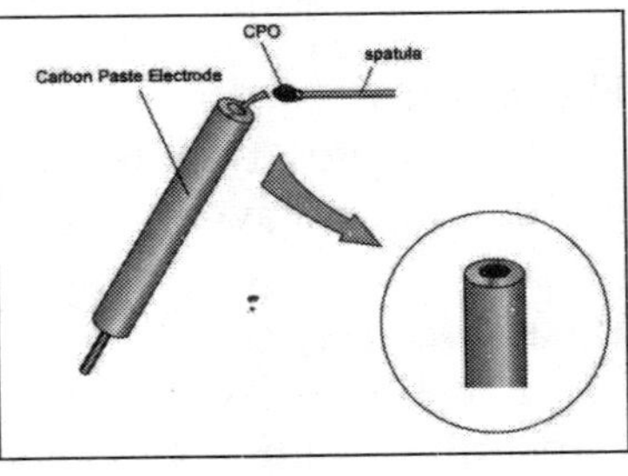

Half cell

Half life

It is the time-period needed for half of a given substance to undergo decay.

Halley's comet

Another name for Comet Halley, it is one of the short-period or periodical comets, which reappears and is seen from Earth approximately after every 75 to 76 years.

Halo

It is a ring of white or coloured light surrounding a luminous body caused by refraction through ice crystals.

Halo nucleus

It refers to an atomic nucleus whose radius is quite larger than that anticipated by the liquid drop model.

Hamiltonian [symbol: H]

It can be described as the operator corresponding to the total energy of the system.

Hard radiation

It can be defined as rays of high-energy and extremely short wavelengths, which are basically electromagnetic radiation, such as high energy X-rays or gamma rays.

Harmonic oscillator

It can refer to any system of periodic oscillating particles that displays harmonic motion, e.g., a pendulum or spring with an attached mass.

Harmonics

It denotes the frequencies of an oscillation or wave.

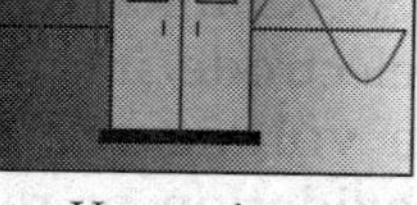

Harmonics

Hassium [Hs]

Produced by atomic collisions, it is an unstable, transuranic, radioactive element with its atomic number as 108.

Health physics

It is the branch of physics that concerns itself with the accurate measurement of agents, such as ionising radiation, and focuses on the health of people working with radioactive materials.

Heat

It is the quantity of energy transferred from one object to another because of a difference in temperature.

Heat capacity

Denoted by a capital C, it can be defined as the number of heat units required to raise or change the temperature of a body by a given amount.

Heat engine

It is an instrument that converts thermal energy (heat) to mechanical energy (work).

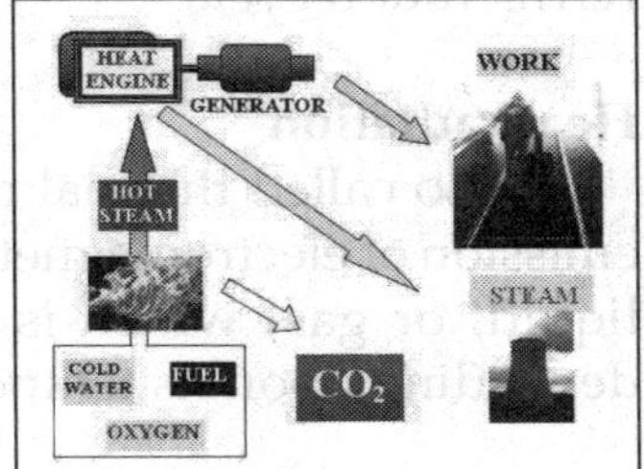

Heat engine

Heat exchanger

It refers to a device which transports heat from one medium (liquid) to another without letting them mix.

Heat of combustion

It is the production of thermal energy when a compound undergoes complete combustion with oxygen.

Heat of fusion

It describes the quantity of energy required to alter a unit mass of a substance from solid to liquid state at the melting point.

Heat of reaction

Also called the enthalpy of reaction, it is the quantity of heat absorbed or released in a chemical reaction.

Heat of solution

It is the amount of heat evolved in the formation of solution that has one mole of solute.

Heat of vapourisation

It can be defined as the quantity of energy required to alter a unit mass of a substance from liquid to gaseous state at the boiling point.

Heat pump

It is a cyclic device that transports heat from a cold area to a heated space with the use of mechanical energy, as in a refrigeration cycle.

Heat radiation

Also called thermal radiation, it is a term used for the emission of electromagnetic radiation from a material (solid, liquid, or gas) which is due to the heat of the material depending upon its temperature.

Heat shield

It refers to the covering or coating on the outside of a spacecraft to shield it from the excessive heat produced when reentering into the earth's atmosphere.

Heat shield

Heat transfer

Another name for heat flow or exchange, it can be described as the movement of heat from one place or point to another.

Heavy water

It is a colourless liquid containing a heavy isotope of hydrogen (deuterium).

Hecto- [symbol: h]

It is a prefix indicating one hundred times.

Heliocentric universe

It refers to the astronomical model of our solar system in which the Earth and other planets revolve around a fixed Sun, which is located at the center of the universe.

Helioseismology

It can be defined as the study of the propagation of wave oscillations and pulsations on the surface of the sun.

Heisenberg uncertainty principle

It denotes that the more accurately one determines the position of a particle, the less accurately the momentum can be known, and vice-versa.

Henry [symbol: H]

It is the SI unit of inductance, which is equal to an electromotive force of one volt in a closed circuit with a uniform rate of change of current of one ampere per second.

Henry's law

It states that the pressure of the gas above a solution is proportional to the concentration of the gas in the solution.

Hertz [symbol: Hz]

It is the SI unit of frequency equal to one event or cycle per second.

Heusler alloys

These are ferromagnetic metal alloys based on a Heusler phase, which are ternanry intermetallic compounds with a specific composition.

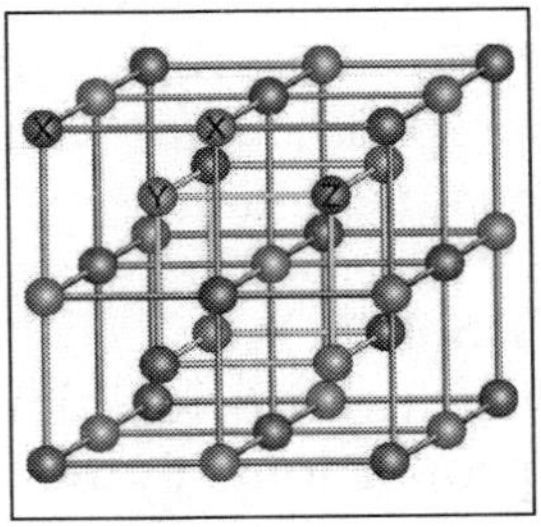

Heusler alloys

Higgs boson

It is an undiscovered massive scalar elementary particle, which predicted to exist by the Standard Model of particle physics.

High frequency

Abbreviated as HF, this relates to the radio frequencies between 3 and 30 megahertz.

Hole

It refers to the absence of an electron in a semi-conductor.

Holographic optical element

Abbreviated as H.O.E., this term can be used for a hologram which consists of a diffraction pattern that is used for managing and controlling transmitted light beams instead of showing images.

Holography

It is the branch of optics that concerns with the study or production of holograms by using a laser's light to generate a 3-d image.

Homopolar generator

Also called unipolar generator, it is a DC electrical generator in which the magnetic field has the same polarity at every point. Its components include an electrically conductive disc rotating in a plane perpendicular to a uniform static magnetic field.

Homopolar generator

Hooke's law

It implies that the deformation of an object is proportional to the force causing it.

Horsepower

Abbreviated as HP, it is the name of units of measuring power. The most common definitions equal between 735.5 and 750 watts.

Hot-wire instrument

It is a device that functions after being expanded by a wire's heat carrying electric current.

Humidity

It can be defined as the atmospheric moisture, which relates to the amount of water vapour in the atmosphere.

Huygens' wavelets

It denotes the model of scattering of waves in which each point on wavefront is the source of circular or spherical waves.

Hydraulic press

It refers to a forcing press with a hydraulically operated ram in which pressure applied by a piston to a small area is transferred through water to another piston having a large area.

Hydraulic system

It includes the machines using fluids to transmit energy, in which a mechanism functions by the resistance offered when a liquid is forced to pass through a small opening, such as pipes, tubes or channels.

Hydraulic system

Hydraulics

It can be defined as the branch of science that deals with the study of the mechanics and conveyance of liquids through small openings for exploring the mechanical properties of fluids.

Hydrodynamics

It can be defined as the branch of science that deals with the study of fluids in motion, which relates to the forces exerted by liquids.

Hydroelectric power

It refers to the energy or electrical power derived from

the kinetic energy of falling water or any other hydraulic means.

Hydrolysis

It is the reaction of substance with water or its ions resulting in its breakdown.

Hydrometeor

It is an atmospheric phenomenon, process, or entity consisting of water or water vapour in various forms, such as rain or a clouds, fog, hail, ice and crystals.

Hydrometer

It is an instrument used to measure the densities of liquids.

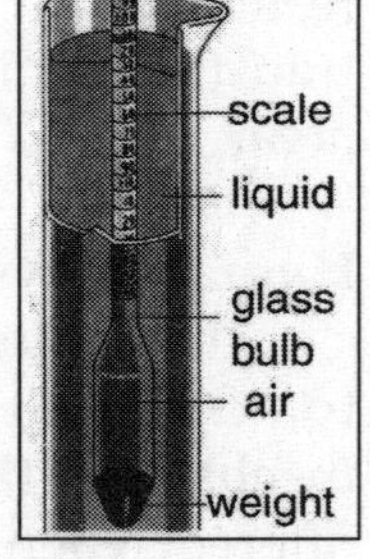

Hydrometer

Hydrostatics

It is that branch of mechanics dealing with the study of hydrostatic properties of liquids, or fluids that are not in motion, or are at rest.

Hygrometer

It refers to an instrument that is used for measuring the relative humidity of the air, or a gas, or the atmosphere.

Hyperbola

It can be defined as the mathematical curve that explains an inverse relationship between two variables.

Hyperfine structure

It describes a range of various effects resulting in shifts in the energy levels of atoms or molecules.

Hypermetropia

Also called as hyperopia, or longsightedness, it describes

a condition or a defect in vision, in which the objects near to the eye are not clearly visible.

Hypernova

Hypernova

It refers to the explosion or gravitational collapse of an extremely massive star at the end of its lifetime to form a black hole.

Hyperon

It can be defined as an unstable subatomic particle such as any baryon, which has mass greater than a neutron and proton.

Hypertonic solution

It refers to a solution with a higher concentration of solute than some other specified solution.

Hypotonic solution

It is a solution of lower osmotic concentration than that of a reference solution or of an isotonic solution.

Hypsometer

It is a term used to define an altimeter that makes use of water's boiling point to indirectly measure and determine land elevation or altitude.

□

I

Ice point

It is the temperature (i) of equilibrium of ice and water at standard pressure; (ii) at which pure water freezes.

Ideal mechanical advantage

It refers to the ratio of effort distance to resistance distance in a machine.

Ideal solution

Also called ideal mixture, it is a solution which follows Raoult's law, in which the enthalpy of a solution is zero.

Ignition temperature

It is the minimum temperature at which combustion takes place spontaneously.

Illuminance

It stands for the rate at which electromagnetic wave energy falls on a surface.

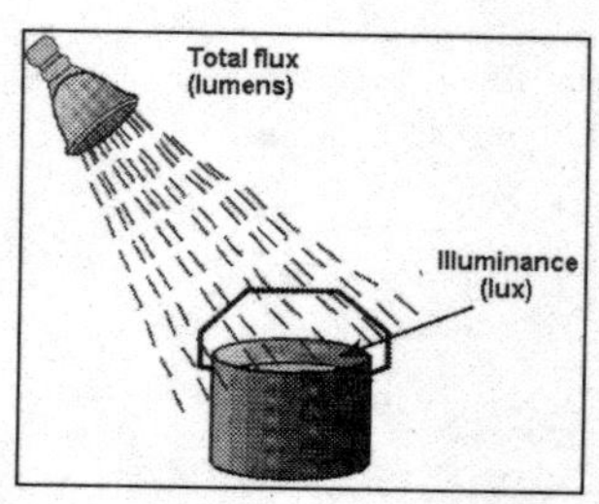

Illuminance

Illuminated object

It is an object on which light falls.

Image

It denotes the reproduction of object created with the use of lenses or mirrors.

Implosion

In this process, the objects are destroyed by collapsing inwardly because of evacuation.

Impulse

It is a product of force and time interval over which it takes place.

Impulse-momentum theorem

It implies that an impulse provided to an object is equal to its alteration in momentum.

Incandescent body

It is an object that has a high temperature, and emits light due to the tremendous heat.

Incident wave

It refers to a particular wave that hits a boundary resulting in either its reflection or refraction.

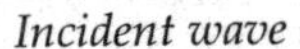

Incident wave

Incoherent light

It stands for the light comprising of waves that are not in step.

Independent variable

It is a kind of variable that can be manipulated or altered when an experiment is taking place.

Index of refraction

It refers to the ratio of the light's speed while travelling in vacuum to its speed while travelling in a material, or an object.

Inelastic collision

It denotes a collision of some kind, in which a particular sort of kinetic energy is transformed into a newer or different form altogether.

Inertia

It explains the disposition of an object to remain inactive and not to change its motion.

Inertia

Inertial mass

It is the ratio of net force applied on an object to its acceleration.

Infrared radiation [IR]

It is an invisible radiation with wavelengths longer than visible light but shorter than radio waves (frequency range between 1 and 430 THz approx.).

Initial velocity

It can be referred to as the velocity of object at time (t = 0).

Instantaneous acceleration

It refers to an acceleration which occurs at a specific time, which can be explained as the slope of tangent to velocity-time graph.

Instantaneous position

It denotes the position of an object at a particular time.

Instantaneous velocity

It is explained as the velocity at a specific time through the use of the slope of the tangent to position-time graph.

Insulator

It is a device containing a material which resists and reduces the flow of electric charge and heat.

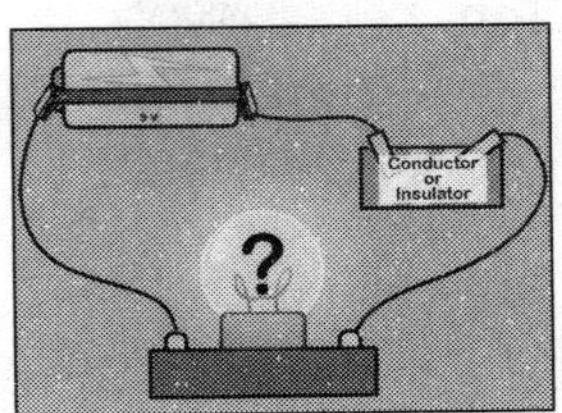

Insulator

Interference fringes

It stands for a pattern of dark and light bands from interference of light waves.

Interference of waves

It refers to the displacements of two or more waves, generating either larger or smaller waves.

Intermolecular forces

It can be explained as those forces that exist between individual particles of a substance.

Internal forces

It can be defined as the forces present between objects within a particular system.

Interstitial compound

This binary compound is formed when an atom of small radius occupies an interstitial space in a metal lattice of another element.

Intrinsic semiconductor

It refers to a type of semiconductor in which conduction takes place by charges not due to impurities, but the host material present in it.

Inverse relationship

It denotes the mathematical relationship between two variables, x and y, which can be summarized by the equation $xy=k$, where k is a constant.

Ion

It is an atom or a group of atoms carrying an electric charge.

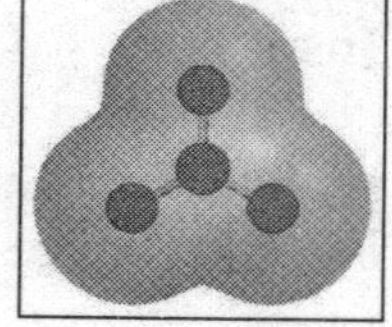

Ion

Ion exchange

It is a phenomenon in which an exchange of ions between an electrolyte solution and a complex (insoluble solid) takes place.

Ionic radius

It is the radius (distance between the centre of the nucleus and the outer edge) of an ion in an ionized state.

Ionic strength

It relates to measuring the concentration of ions and strength of an electric field in a given solution.

Ionisation

It is a process of ionising, in which dissociation of atoms occurs due to chemical reaction or radiation.

Ionising radiation

It can be defined as those particles or waves that can separate electrons from atoms, and remove molecules or atoms from a solid.

Isoelectronic

It refers to two or more entities with the same number of electrons or similar electronic structure but consisting of different elements.

Isolated system

It is a collection of objects, not acted upon by external forces, into which energy neither comes in nor retreats.

Isomerism

It refers to the condition of being an isomer.

Isomers

These are substances or compounds with the same molecular weight but different structural formula.

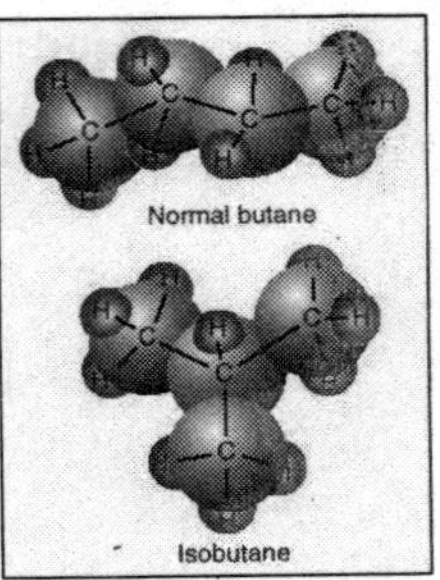

Isomers

Isomorphism

It refers to the similarity in appearance (form or shape) but genetically different.

Isotherm

It is a (i) curve displaying changes in volume and pressure at a constant temperature; (ii) line linking locations having the same temperature at a given point.

Isotopes

These are radioactive forms of an element that have different numbers of neutrons in the nuclei and, therefore, differ in relative atomic mass. These forms have atomic nuclei with same number of protons but different numbers of neutrons.

Isotropic

It refers to a physical property of a substance possessing the same value when measured in any direction.

IUPAC

It is known as the International Union of Pure and Applied Chemistry.

□

J

Jahn-Teller effect

Named after Hermann Arthur Jahn and Edward Teller, it refers to the geometrical distortion of non-linear molecules under specific conditions.

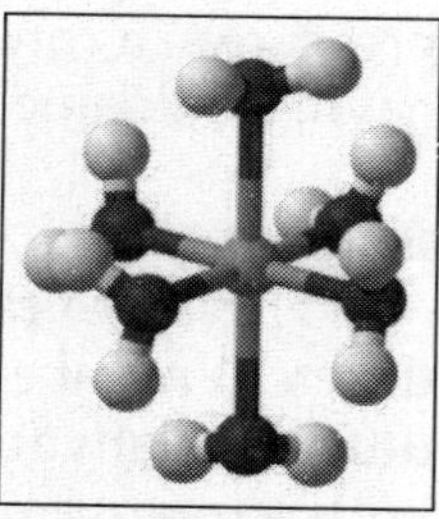

Jahn-Teller effect

j-j coupling

This mechanism is used when the spin-orbit interaction is powerful in comparison to the electrostatic interaction.

Joule [symbol: J]

It is a unit of energy in the SI system equal to one Newton-meter.

Joule heating

It can be explained as temperature's increase of electrical conductor due to conversion of electrical to thermal energy.

□

K

Katharometer

It is a device used for measuring thermal conductivity.

Kelvin temperature scale

It is a type of temperature scale in which 0 K is equal to absolute zero, and 273.16 K is equal to triple point of water.

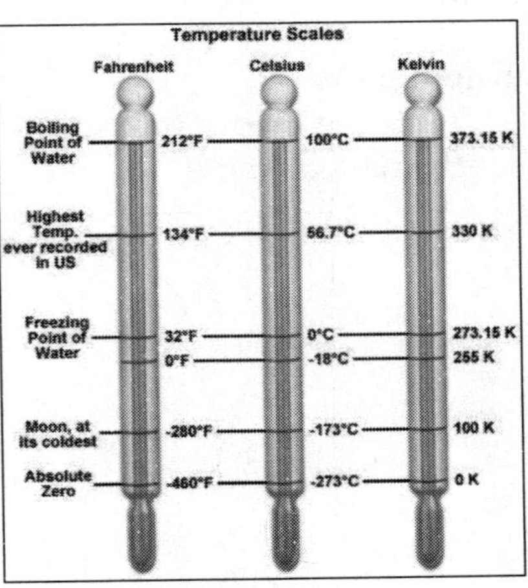

Kelvin temperature scale

Kepler's laws

These can be defined as the three laws of motion of bodies drawn together by the force of gravitation.

Kilogram [symbol: kg]

It is the SI unit used for assessing mass.

Kilowatt hour

It refers to the amount of energy equal to $\text{kWh} = (3600\text{s})(\text{kW}) = 3600\text{s}\left(\frac{\text{kJ}}{\text{s}}\right) = 3600\text{kJ}$ and it is generally applied in electrical measurement.

Kinematics

It can be explained as the study of motion of objects without taking into consideration the reasons for this motion.

Kinetic energy

It is the mechanical energy that matter has due to its motion.

Kinetic-molecular energy

It is a description of matter as being built of extremely minute particles in constant motion.

Kinetics

It is the study about the forces that lead to the movement or motion of bodies.

Knot theory

It is the theory that studies, classifies and disentangles mathematical knots.

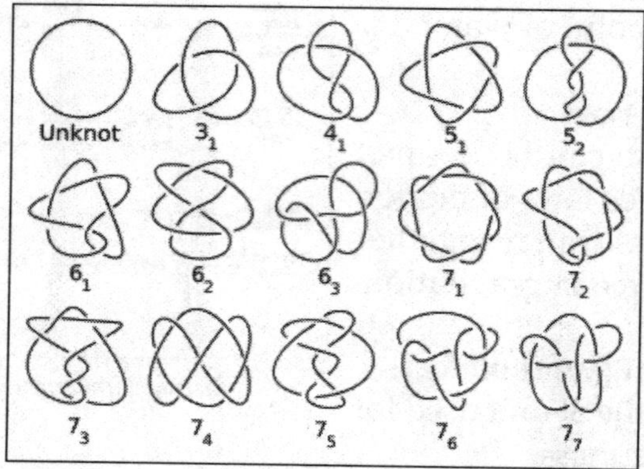

Knot theory

Kovar

It is an alloy of iron, nickel and cobalt with thermal expansion properties, and is used as an electroplated conductor in electronic parts.

□

Langmuir-Blodgett film

It is a set of monolayers, or layers of organic material, one molecule thick, accumulated on a solid substratum.

Laser

It is an acronym for a device that produces a strong beam of coherent monochromatic light by stimulated emission of radiation.

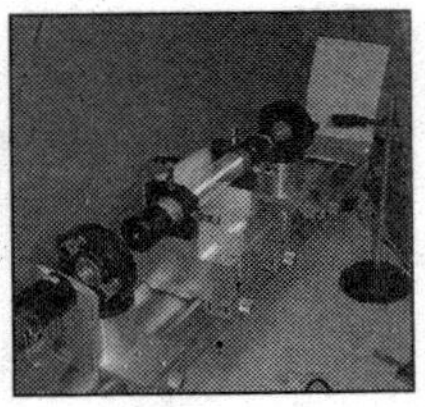

Laser

Laser-induced fusion

It can be summed as a proposed way of generating nuclear fusion by the use of heating produced by intense laser beams to thrust and squeeze matter together.

Latent heat

It is the heat which is released or absorbed by a substance during a change of phase without any temperature change.

Law of conservation of energy

It is a law which states that the total momentum in a closed, isolated system remains constant.

Law of reflection

This law states that the angle of incidence of a wave is equal to the angle of reflection.

Law of universal gravitation

It is a law stating that the gravitational force existing between two objects depends directly upon the product of their masses, and inversely on the square of their separation.

Lawrencium [Lr]

This transuranic, radioactive metallic element of the actinide series, with its atomic number as 103, is synthesized from californium.

Leclanche cell

It is a common type of dry voltaic cell that produces approximately 1.5 volts.

Lens

It is an optical device made for converging or diverging light.

Lens

Lenz's law

It refers to the magnetic field produced by an induced current which resists the alteration in the field that caused the current.

Lepton

It can be defined as that particle that goes on to take up interactions with other particles specifically by the electroweak and gravitational interactions.

Lever arm

It is a component of the displacement of the force from the axis of rotation in the axis of rotation in the direction perpendicular to the force.

Light

It can be referred to as an electromagnetic radiation, which is visible, and has its wavelengths between 400 and 700 nm.

Limiting reactant

It is a substance that stoichiometrically limits the amount of product(s) that can be produced.

Linear accelerator

It is an instrument used for accelerating charged subatomic particles along a straight line path by applying successive electric field.

Linear relationship

It points towards the relationship between two variables, x and y, summarized by the equation y = ax + b, where a and b are constant.

Linear restoring force

It is a kind of force in direction towards the equilibrium position that depends linearly on distance from distance from that position.

Line spectrum

It is an atomic emission or absorption spectrum.

Liquid

It can be summed up as those materials that have fixed volume, but have the flexibility to take any shape, depending on the shape of the container.

Liquid crystal

It is a substance exhibiting properties of both solid and liquid, and is used in cameras, mobile phones, etc.

Lithium battery

It is a rechargeable battery having lithium metal or compounds as its anode.

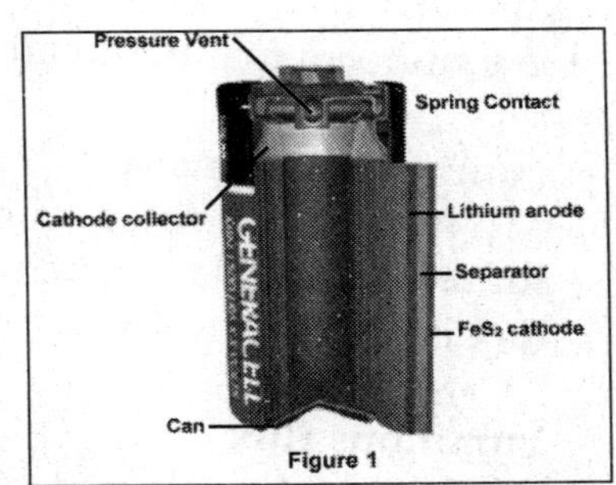

Lithium battery

Lodestone

Another name for loadstone, this naturally occurring magnetic rock consists of magnetite that possesses polarity.

Lodestone

Longitudinal waves

It is a kind of wave in which direction of disturbance is similar to the direction of wave's travel.

Loudness

It is a physiological measure or magnitude of a sound wave's amplitude, which is heard on pitch and tone colour along with amplitude.

Lumen [symbol: lm]

It denotes a unit of luminous flux which equals to the amount of light emitted through a solid angle of one steradian by a point source of one candela intensity beaming in a uniform manner in all directions.

Luminance intensity

It can be defined as a measure of light given out by source in candelas, which is calculated when the luminous flux is divided by 4pie.

Luminous flux

It can be explained as the flux or flow of light from a particular source, which is measured in lumens.

Luminous object

It is referred to as an object that gives out or exudes light, and is unlike an object that reflects light.

Lux [symbol: lx]

It is the SI unit of illuminance and luminous emittance, which is one lumen per square meter.

□

M

Machine

It is a mechanical or electrical device that changes force or energy needed to carry out work for performing of human tasks.

Machine

Macroscopic

It is something which is sufficiently large to be visible to the naked eye.

Magnadur

This ceramic material consisting of sintered iron oxide and barium is used for manufacturing permanent magnets.

Magnalium

This common alloy is mainly a mixture of aluminium and magnesium finds its use in engineering, making fireworks, etc.

Magnetic field

It is a kind of space around a magnet within which magnetic force exists.

Magnetism

Generated by the movement of electric charge, this physical phenomenon leads to attractive and repulsive forces between objects.

Magnetochemistry

It is a chemistry that analyses the effect of a magnetic field on molecular structure.

Magnification

It is the ratio of size of an optical image to the size of the object.

Manipulated variable

It is a type of variable that the experimenter can manipulate or change.

Manometer

It is a two-armed barometer (pressure gauge) for comparing pressures of a gas.

Manometer

Maser

It is an acronym for microwave amplification by stimulated emission of coherent radiation, such as in a laser.

Mass

Generally measured in grams and kilograms, it is a measure of the amount of matter in an object.

Mass action

It is the concept in which a large number of atoms reacting randomly by themselves can form a larger pattern.

Mass defect

It can be defined as the mass equivalent of the binding energy, which can be summarized as $m=E/C^2$.

Mass number

It can be referred to as the number of nucleons (protons plus neutrons) present in the nucleus of an atom.

Mass spectrometer

It is a kind of instrument used for measuring the atomic or molecular mass.

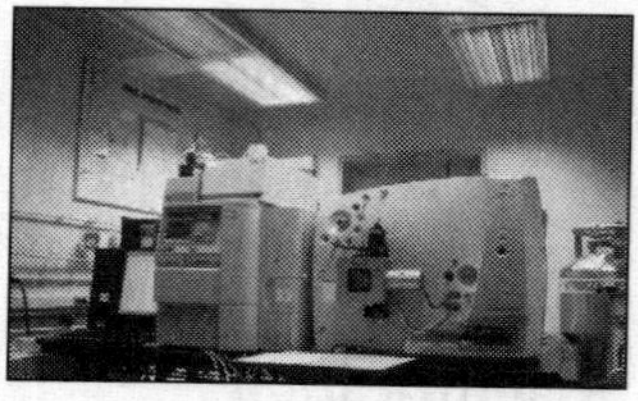

Mass spectrometer

Mass spectroscopy

This spectroscopy is an analytical method to measure the masses of small electrically charged particles.

Matrix

It is the main constituent of a composite material.

Matter wave

It can be explained as the wave-like properties of particles, such as the one present in electrons.

Mechanical advantage

It refers to the ratio of resistance force to effort force in a machine.

Mechanical energy

It can be defined as the aggregate of potential and kinetic energies.

Mechanical resonance

It denotes a condition at which natural oscillation frequency equals frequency of driving force, and where the amplitude of oscillatory motion reaches its maximum.

Mechanical wave

It is a type of wave comprising of periodic motion of

matter, such as sound wave or water wave which is unlike electromagnetic wave.

Meitnerium [Mt]

Produced by atomic collisions, this unstable, radioactive, transuranic element of atomic number 109 is used in nuclear fissions.

Melting point

Also called the freezing point, it is the temperature at which liquid and solid are in equilibrium.

Mercury cell

Also called mercury battery, this primary cell is an electrochemical battery that cannot be recharged.

Mercury cell

Meson

It is referred to as a medium mass subatomic particle made up by combining quark and antiquark.

Metallurgy

It describes the complete processes of extracting metals from ores.

Metastable state

It is an excited stationary energy state of an atom with an unusually long lifetime.

Meter [symbol: m]

It is the SI unit used to determine and measure length.

Micro-

It is a prefix meaning one millionth.

Microscopic

It is something which is so minute that it cannot be seen with a naked eye, and becomes visible only with the help of a microscope.

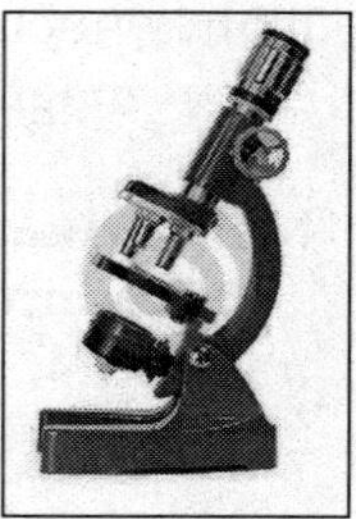

Microscopic

Microwaves

These electromagnetic waves have wavelengths shorter than a radio wave but longer than an infrared wave.

Mirror equation

It can be summarized as: 1/do +1/di=1/f, where do is object distance, di is image distance and f is focal length.

Moderator

It is a substance or material, which is used to inhibit and decrease speed of neutrons in nuclear reactor.

Molar

It is assigning a solution consisting of one mole of solute per litre of solution.

Molar conductivity

It describes the conductivity of an electrolyte solution divided by the molar concentration of the electrolyte, determining the efficiency of an electrolyte to conduct electricity.

Molar heat capacity

It is the amount of heat energy required to raise the temperature of one mole of a substance.

Molar volume

Also called molecular volume, it is the volume occupied by one mole of a substance at a given temperature and pressure.

Mole

It can be defined as the SI unit of molecular weight of a substance measured in grams.

Molecular formula

It refers to a formula that shows the actual number of atoms present in a molecule of a substance.

Molecular sieve

It is a crystalline material containing pores of a precise and uniform size, allowing the passage of molecules below a certain size.

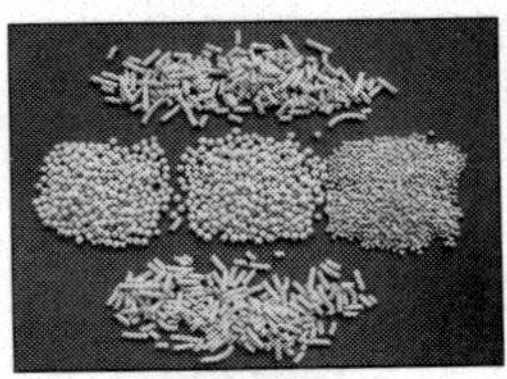

Molecular sieve

Molecular weight

It is the mass of one molecule of a non-ionic substance in atomic mass units.

Molecule

It is the smallest particle of a substance which can exist independently.

Mole fraction

It is the number of moles of a component of a mixture divided by the total number of moles in the mixture.

Momentum

It can refer to the product of an object's mass and velocity.

Monochromatic light

It is a kind of light which has a single, or one wavelength.

Multiplet

It is a class of closely associated things, such as atomic energy levels.

Mutarotation

It is the change in optical rotation of a sugar seen right after it dissolves in a liquid solution.

Myopia

It can simply be called nearsightedness, a defect of eye, in which distant objects focus in front of the retina and, thus, appear blurred.

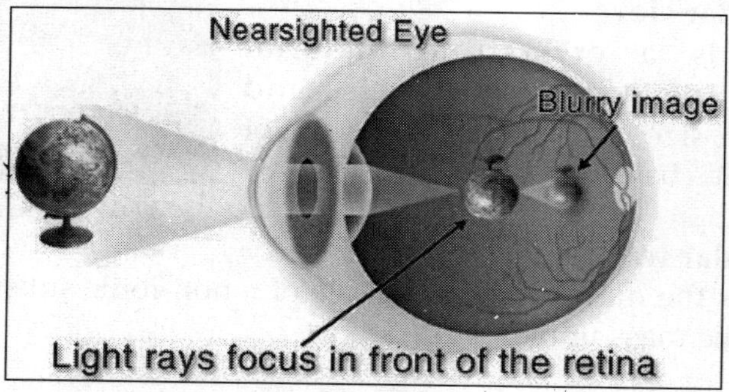

Myopia

□

N

n-type semiconductor

It is a kind of semiconductor in which current is carried by electrons.

Nano-

It is a prefix which means one-billionth.

Nanotechnology

This type of technology relates to the dimensions of things which are less than a hundred nanometers.

Nematic crystal

Nematic crystal

It is a kind of translucent liquid crystal in which the waves pass through the liquid and lead the polarisation of light waves to change.

Neptunium [Np]

Obtained artificially and naturally, it is a radioactive, transuranic metallic element of the actinide series with its atomic number as 93.

Net force

It can be described as the vector sum of forces on an object.

Neutral

It is an object or material that has no net electric charge.

Neutrino

It can be referred to as a subatomic particle without charge and mass (a type of lepton) which is emitted with beta particles.

Neutron

It is a neutral subatomic particle which is a kind of nucleon with no charge and mass slightly greater than that of proton (1.0087 amu).

Neutron diffraction

It is a technique by which neutrons are used to ascertain the atomic and magnetic structure of a substance.

Newton

It is the SI unit of force equal to the force that provides an acceleration of 1 m s^{-2} to a mass of 1 kilogram.

Newton's law of motion

These can be summed as the laws relating to force and acceleration.

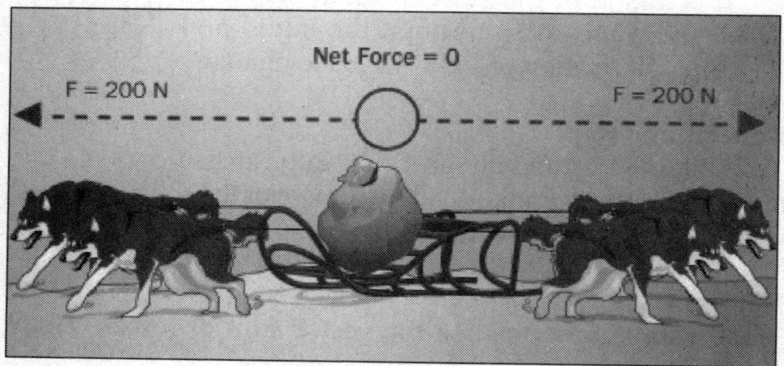

Newton's law of motion

Nobelium [No]

Obtained by bombarding curium with carbon ions, it is a radioactive, transuranic, synthetic metallic element of the actinide series with its atomic number as 102.

Node

It can be denoted as the point where disruptions due to two or more waves lead to no displacement.

Non-metal

It is an element which lacks the chemical or physical properties of a metal.

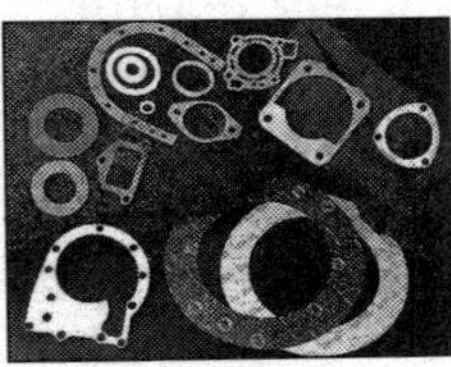

Non-metal

Non-polar compound

This compound is equal and neutral, without a net charge.

Normal

It can be explained as being perpendicular to plane of interest.

Normal force

It is described as a force perpendicular to surface.

Nuclear equation

It is an equation which signifies the workings of a nuclear reaction.

Nuclear fission

It is a nuclear reaction in which a heavy nucleus splits into nuclei of intermediate masses simultaneously releasing energy.

Nuclear fusion

It is a kind of reaction in which two nuclei are integrated and combined into one.

Nuclear magnetic resonance

Abbreviated as NMR, it is a property relating to the resonance of protons to radiation in a magnetic field.

Nuclear reaction

It is a process which changes the composition, structure of a nucleus and evolves or absorbs large amount of energy.

Nuclear reactor

It is a device in which nuclear fusion is used to generate electric current.

Nuclear transmutation

It can be defined as the change of one nucleus into another due to a nuclear reaction.

Nucleons

These can be referred to as the particles comprising the nucleus (proton or neutron).

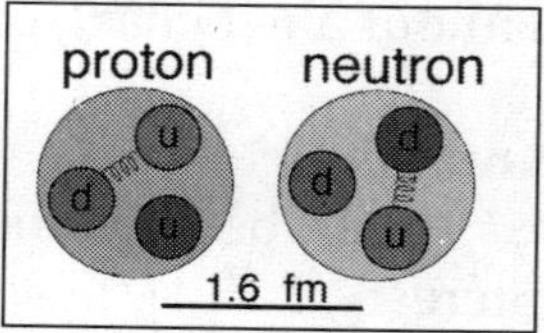

Nucleons

Nucleosynthesis

It is the phenomenon of forming new atomic nuclei from the pre-existing nucleons.

Nucleus

It is a minute, dense, positively charged centre of an atom comprising of protons, neutrons and other particles.

Nuclide

It describes an atomic species in contrast to isotopes, which refer only to different atomic forms of a single element.

□

O

Object

It can be described as the source of diverging light rays, which can be either luminous or illuminated.

Occultation

It can be defined as an occurrence when one celestial body conceals or obscures another, e.g., when the Sun is hidden by the Moon during a solar eclipse, then it is an occultation.

Occultation

Octane number

It is a number which points to the anti-knock properties of a fuel.

Octave

It can be defined as the interval between two frequencies with a ratio of two to one.

Octet

It is a stable group of eight electrons with a single shell in an atom.

Ohm

It is the SI unit of electrical resistance, which equals to one volt per ampere.

Ohmmeter

It is a device for measuring electrical resistance in ohms.

Ohm's law

It denotes that the resistance of an object is constant, and is independent of voltage across it.

Opaque

It is an object or material that does not transmit or reflect light.

Opaque

Opacity

It can be referred to as the phenomenon of not permitting the passage of electromagnetic radiation or other kinds of radiations, mainly visible light.

Opalescence

Used as a synonym for iridescence, it refers to a kind of dichroism, which is seen in highly dispersed systems with little opacity.

Open-pipe resonator

It refers to a cylindrical tube with its both ends closed and a sound source at one end.

Opposition

It can be defined as the apparent position of two celestial objects that are directly opposite to each other in the sky, esp. when a superior planet is opposite to the sun.

Optical activity

It can stand for the rotation of plane polarised light by one of a pair of optical isomers.

Optical fibre

It is an extremely thin fibre or wire, which is made from

glass and transparent plastics, and is primarily used in networks for transmitting information optically with very low error rates.

Optical glass

It is a kind of clear, homogeneous, pure glass of known refractive index used for lenses.

Optical isomers

Another name for enantiomers, these are stereoisomers that differ only by being nonsuperimposable mirror images of each other.

Optical microscope

Also known as light microscope, it can be defined as a type of microscope using visible light, typically viewed directly by the eye.

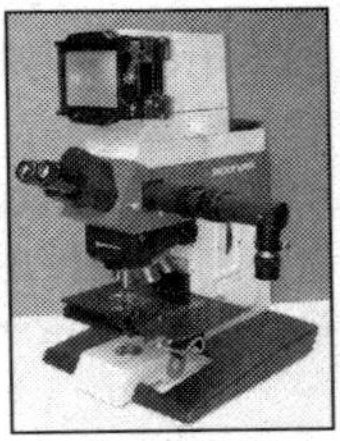

Optical microscope

Optical pyrometer

Also called brightness pyrometer, it is a non-contact temperature measurement device, which uses a narrow band of radiation within the visible range (0.4 to 0.7 microns) to measure temperature by colour matching and other techniques.

Optical tweezers

These are scientific instruments that use a highly focused laser beam to provide an attractive or repulsive force, depending on the refractive index mismatch to physically hold and move microscopic dielectric objects.

Orbit

It can be referred to as the curved path of a celestial object or spacecraft around a star, planet, or moon, esp. a periodic elliptical revolution.

Orbital

It is the pattern of electron density that may be formed in a molecule.

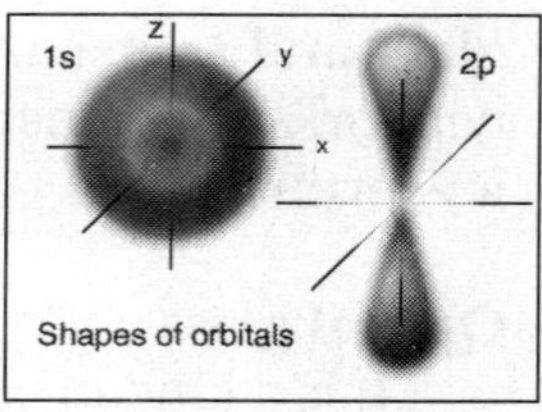

Orbital

Order

It is the order of reaction described as the power to which its concentration term in the rate equation is raised.

Ortho-

It is a prefix denoting substitution at two adjacent carbon atoms in a benzene ring.

Oscillation

It refers to the regular variation in magnitude or position around a central point.

Oscillator

It is defined as a device for generating oscillating electric currents or voltages by non-mechanical means.

Oscillatory universe

Also known as a cyclic model, it refers to any of several cosmological models in which the universe follows infinite, self-sustaining cycles.

Osmiridium

A natural alloy of osmium and iridium, this rare, hard, corrosion-resistant mineral is used in needles, pen nibs, munitions, etc.

Osmometer

It is a device for measuring osmotic pressure or strength of a solution.

Osmosis

It is the process in which molecules of a solvent move through a semipermeable membrane from a dilute solution into a more concentrated solution.

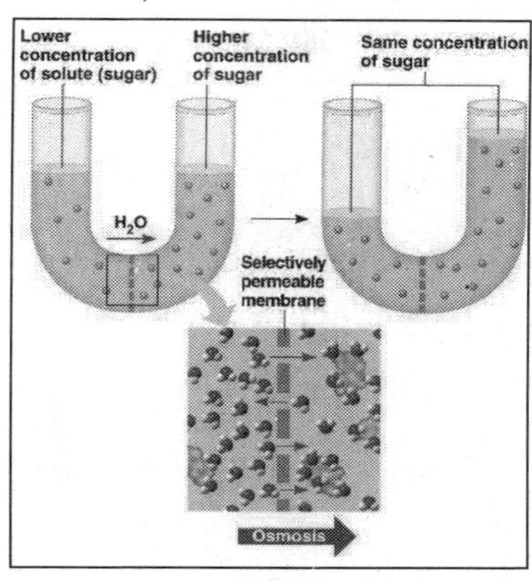

Osmosis

Osmotic pressure

It is the hydrostatic pressure generated on the surface of a semi-permeable membrane as a result of osmosis.

Ostwald ripening

It is a phenomenon occurring in solutions (solid or liquid), explaining the alteration of an inhomogeneous structure over time.

Ostwald's dilution law

This law states a relationship between the dissociation constant and the degree of dissociation of a weak electrolyte.

Overpotential

It refers to the difference between a half-reaction's thermodynamic and observed potentials.

Ozone [O_3]

Formed from oxygen, this colourless, poisonous gas is a strong oxidising agent, and acts as a screen for ultraviolet radiation.

Ozone layer

It is a layer in the earth's stratosphere at an altitude of about 10 km (6.2 miles) containing a high concentration of ozone, which absorbs most of the ultraviolet radiation reaching the earth from the sun.

p-type semiconductor

It can be defined as a kind of semiconductor in which conduction is the result of motion of holes.

Pair production

It is the formation of particle and antiparticle from gamma rays.

Palaeomagnetism

It can be defined as the study of the record of the Earth's magnetic field in rocks. Some minerals in rocks can record direction of the field as it has altered over geologic time.

Palaeomagnetism

Para-

It is a prefix indicating substitution at diametrically opposite carbon atoms in a benzene ring.

Parabolic mirror

It can be referred to as a mirror having the shape of a paraboloid of revolution that has no spherical aberration.

Parallel circuit

It is defined as a circuit in which there are two or more paths through which the current can flow.

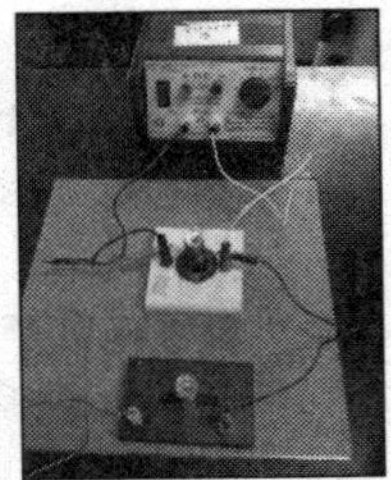
Parallel circuit

Parallel connection

It means a connection of two or more electrical devices between two points to provide more than one current path.

Paramagnetism

It refers to the attraction towards a magnetic field, weaker than ferromagnetism and stronger than diamagnetism.

Paraxial ray

Mainly used in the context of geometric optics, the paraxial approximation is a small-angle approximation applied in ray tracing of light by the use of an optical system.

Partial pressure

It is the pressure exerted by one gas in a mixture of gases.

Particle

It is referred to as a hypothetical object having mass but no physical size or dimensions.

Partition coefficient

It is the ratio of the concentrations of a solute in two immiscible substances at equilibrium.

Pascal

It is the SI unit of pressure, which is one neutron per square meter.

Pascal's principle

It can be defined as the pressure applied to a fluid is transmitted undiminished throughout it.

Paschen-Back effect

It is a splitting of spectral lines seen when the source of a radiation is in the presence of a strong magnetic field.

Paschen series

It is a series of lines in the infrared spectrum of atomic hydrogen.

Peculiar motion

Also known as peculiar velocity, it can be defined as the true velocity of an object, relative to a rest frame.

Pendulum

It refers to a setup in which a weight is hung from a fixed point so that it can swing freely backward and forward, which is usually used in a clock for regulating its mechanism.

Penning gauge

It is defined as a cold cathode ionisation gauge consisting of two electrodes anode and cathode.

Perihelion

It refers to the position in a heliocentric orbit at which the orbiting object is at its least distance from the Sun.

Period

It is the time needed to repeat one complete cycle of motion.

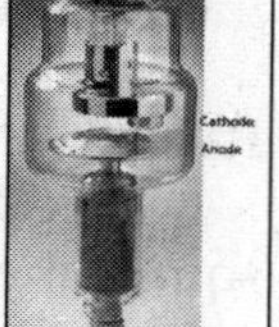

Periodic law

This law states that the properties of the elements are periodic functions of their atomic numbers.

Periodic law

Periodic motion

It is a kind of motion that repeats itself at regular intervals of time.

Periodic table

It is an arrangement of elements according to the increasing atomic numbers based on the periodic law.

Peripheral device

It refers to the hardware, outside or inside the case or housing for the essential computer, that is capable of providing input to the essential computer or of receiving output or of both.

Periscope

It is an instrument for observation from a concealed position, or provides a vision of otherwise an obstructed sight.

Periscope

Permalloys

It is a term for a nickel-iron magnetic alloy with about 20% iron and 80% nickel content. These are known to have a high magnetic permeability, low coercivity, near zero magnetostriction, and significant anisotropic magnetoresistance.

Permanent gas

It is a gas at a pressure and temperature which is incapable of liquefaction.

Permanent magnet

It can be defined as a magnet which retains its property of magnetism for an indefinite period.

Perturbation

It refers to a minor disturbance in the course of a celestial body, caused by the gravitational attraction of a neighbouring body.

Petroleum

Found and extracted from rock strata beneath the earth's

surface, this poisonous, flammable liquid mixture of hydrocarbons of various molecular weights is refined for the production of other fuels.

Pewter

It is an alloy of tin and lead that produces a metal with a dull gray appearance. It is used for tablewares and other small objects copying silver forms.

Pewter

Pfund series

It is the series denoting the emission spectrum of hydrogen when the electron is jumping to the fifth orbital.

Phase

It is a distinct state (solid, liquid or gaseous) of matter in a chemical system.

Phase diagram

It displays the equilibrium temperature-pressure relationships for different phases of a substance.

Phase rule

It states the maximum number of phases, constituents, and degrees of freedom possible in a system.

Phonochemistry

It is the branch of chemistry related to the effects of sound and ultrasonic waves on chemical reactions.

Photocathode

It refers to a negatively charged electrode in a light detection device such as a photomultiplier or phototube that is coated with a photosensitive compound.

Photochemical reaction

This reaction takes place by the action or absorption of light.

Photochemistry

It is a branch of chemistry concerned with the action or effect of light on chemical systems.

Photochromism

It is the reversible transformation of a material between two forms when exposed to electromagnetic radiation.

Photodisintegration

It refers to a phenomenon that takes place when a high-energy photon is absorbed by an atomic nucleus.

Photoelasticity

This optical method is used to determine and evaluate stress distribution in a material, using a transparent model of a part, or a thick film of photoelastic material bonded to a real part.

Photoelectric cell

It is a kind of a cell whose electrical properties change when light falls on it. Such cells are used in camera light meters, television camera tubes, and automatic detection devices.

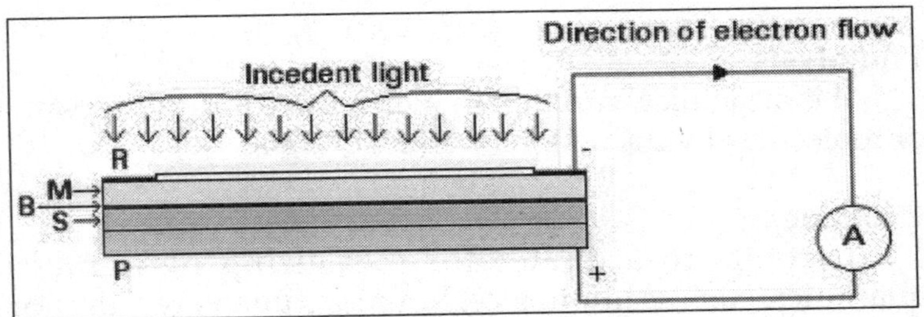

Photoelectric cell

Photoelectric effect

It can be referred to as the election of electrons from surface of metal exposed to electromagnetic radiation.

Photoelectron

It is defined as a type of electron emitted from an atom by interaction with a photon, especially an electron emitted from a solid surface by the action of light.

Photoemission

It is the process of emitting electrons from a surface due to the action of light striking it.

Photofission

In this phenomenon, a nucleus, after absorbing a gamma ray, undergoes nuclear fission (splits into two fragments of nearly equal mass).

Photography

It is a process of generating images of objects by recording radiation on a radiation-sensitive medium, such as a photographic film, or an electronic sensor.

Photography

Photoionisation

This process is generated in a medium by the action of electromagnetic radiation, where an incident photon releases one or more electrons from a molecule.

Photolysis

It is a chemical reaction in which there is decomposition of molecules by the action or effect of light.

Photometer

It refers to a device for measuring photometric quantities, such as luminance, luminous intensity, luminous flux, and illuminance.

Photometry

It is the science of the measurement of light and its properties, in terms of its perceived brightness to the human eye.

Photomicrography

It is the art of doing photography by using a microscope to show a magnified image of an item.

Photomultiplier

It is an instrument in which incident photons create measurable electrical pulses or signals, and is also used device for detecting photons.

Photon

Also called quantum of light, it can be defined as a packet of light or electromagnetic radiation.

Photonics

It is the branch of technology concerned with the properties and transmission of photons, which includes the generation, emission, transmission, modulation, signal processing, switching, amplification, detection and sensing of light.

Photosphere

It refers to that region of an astronomical object from which externally received light originates.

Photosynthesis

This process generally occurring in plants involves synthesis of compounds with the help of light, in which oxygen is generated as a byproduct.

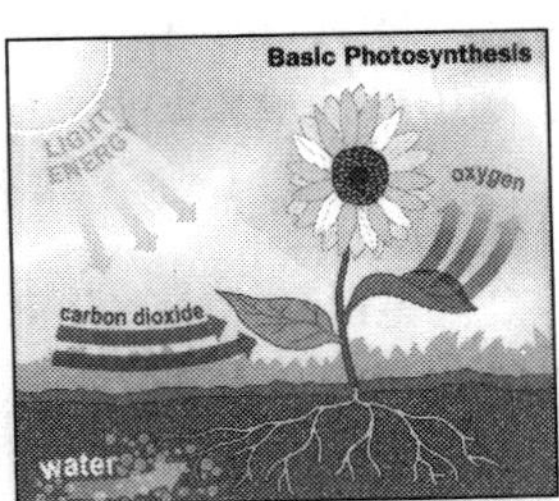

Photosynthesis

Phototransistor

It is a type of transistor that responds to light striking it by generating and amplifying an electric current.

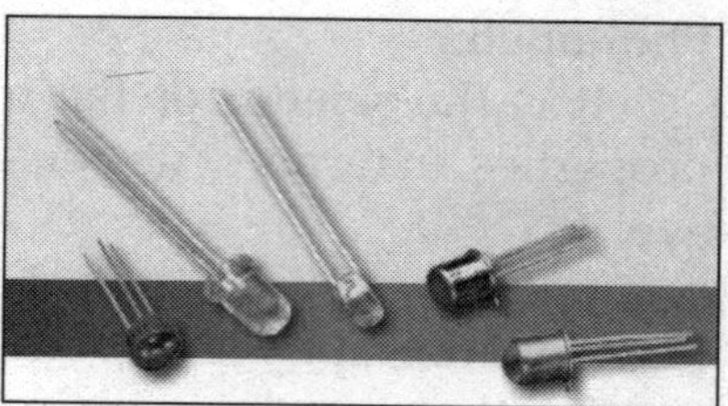
Phototransistor

Photovoltaic cell

It refers to a particular device that converts electromagnetic radiation into electrical energy.

pH scale

It is a way of measuring acidity and alkalinity of a substance, where = 7 is neutral, < 7 is more basic, and > 7 is more acidic.

Physical chemistry

The branch of chemistry concerned with the physical properties of chemical substances.

Physics

It can be defined as the study of matter and energy and the relationship that exists between the two.

Pi electron

It is an electron involved in a pi bond.

Piezoelectricity

It refers to the electric potential that is generated by deforming material.

Pig iron

Also called Cast Iron, it is iron with high carbon content, making it hard but brittle. Pig iron is crude iron as first obtained from a blast furnace, in the form of oblong blocks.

Pigment

It can be defined as a coloured material that absorbs certain colours and transmits or reflects others.

Pion

It is a meson having a mass approximately 270 times that of an electron.

Pitch

It is referred to as perceived sound characteristics, which are equivalent to frequency.

Pitot tube

It is defined as a sensor to measure fluid velocity by generating a pressure that is the difference between the total static pressure and the dynamic pressure.

Pixel

It refers to a minute area of illumination on a display screen, one of many from which an image is made of.

Planck's constant [symbol: h]

It is the ratio of energy of photon to its frequency.

Plane mirror

It is a kind of mirror which is flat, and has a smooth surface that reflects light continually.

Planet

It is a celestial body orbiting a star or stellar remnant that is massive enough to be rounded by its own gravity, is not massive enough to cause thermonuclear fusion, and has cleared its neighbouring region of planetesimals.

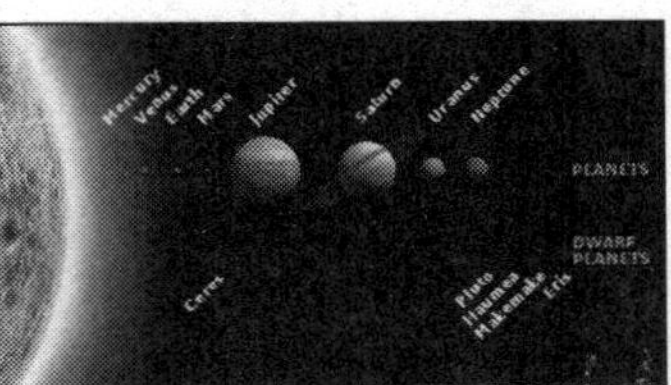

Planet

Planimeter

Invented in 1894 by British mathematician O. Henrici, it is a device for mechanically measuring the area of a plane figure.

Plasma

It means the state of matter in which atoms are separated into electrons and positive ions or bare nuclei.

Plasma display

It refers to a screen-display technology that uses ionised gas (plasma) to create an image. In some plasma devices, the light emitted by the plasma is used to stimulate a phosphor, which then gives out visible light.

Plasma display

Plasmonics

It can be defined as a proposed analogy to electronics using plasmons.

Plasticity

It is the property of a solid body whereby it undergoes a permanent change in shape or size when subjected to a stress exceeding the yield value.

Plutonium [Pu]

Naturally occurring in small quantities in uranium ores and mostly manufactured in nuclear reactors, this solid, dense, silvery radioactive metallic element of the actinide series of atomic number 94, is used as a fuel, explosive, etc.

Point object

It is a particular kind of object idealized as so small to be located at only one position.

Poison

It is a chemical substance that (i) inhibits another substance or a reaction; (ii) can be harmful and even fatal if consumed by chemical means.

Poison

Polarimeter

It is an instrument used to measure optical activity.

Polarization

It is defined as the process in which waves of light or other radiation are restricted in direction of vibration.

Polarised light

It can be defined as the light in which electric fields are all in the same plane.

Polar molecule

It is a type of molecule with a pair of electric charges of opposite polarity, such as water, ammonia, etc.

Polaroid

It is a plastic film that generates a high degree of plane polarisation in light passing through it, and is used in sunglasses.

Pollution

It is the introduction of contaminants into a natural environment that causes instability, disorder, damage or discomfort to the ecosystem i.e. physical systems or living organisms.

Polonium [Po]

Naturally found in uranium ores, this rare, radioactive metallic element of atomic number 84, includes heaters in space probes, antistatic devices, etc.

Polychromatic radiation

It is a kind of electromagnetic radiation that consists of two or more frequencies or wavelengths.

Polyhedron

It refers to a solid figure with many flat faces and straight edges.

Position

It means the separation between object and a reference point.

Position-time graph

It is the graph of object's motion that shows how its position depends on clock reading, or time.

Positron

It implies an antiparticle, which is equivalent of electron.

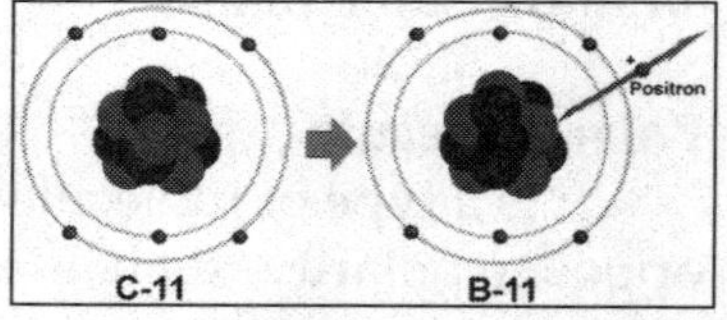

Positron

Positronium

It is defined as a system consisting of an electron and its anti-particle, a positron, bound together into an "exotic atom".

Potential barrier

It is a region within a force field in which the potential is significantly higher than at points on either side of it, so that a particle requires energy to pass through it.

Potential difference

It can be defined as a difference in electric potential between two points.

Potential energy

It is the energy of an object due to its position or state.

Potentiometer

It can be referred to as an electrical device with a variable resistance, for instance, rheostat.

Powder metallurgy

It refers to the art of producing metal powders and of utilizing metal powders for the production of massive materials and shaped objects.

Power

It is the rate of doing work, which is also referred to as the rate of energy conversion.

Preamplifier

It is a kind of amplifier used to increase the output of a low level source allowing the signal to be processed by other devices.

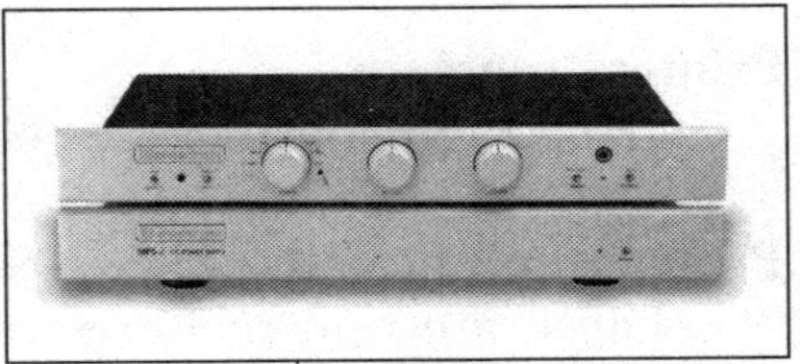

Preamplifier

Precipitation

It refers to the action of forming a chemical solid by precipitating a substance in a solution or solid.

Precision

It is the degree of exactness in a measurement.

Presbyopia

It is a health condition where the eye exhibits a progressively diminished ability to focus on near objects with age.

Pressure [symbol: P]

It is the amount of the force applied to a unit area of surface, which is measured in pascals.

Pressure gauge

It is a kind of gauge for measuring and indicating fluid pressure.

Primary coil

It can be defined as the transformer coil that, when connected to voltage source, produces varying magnetic flux.

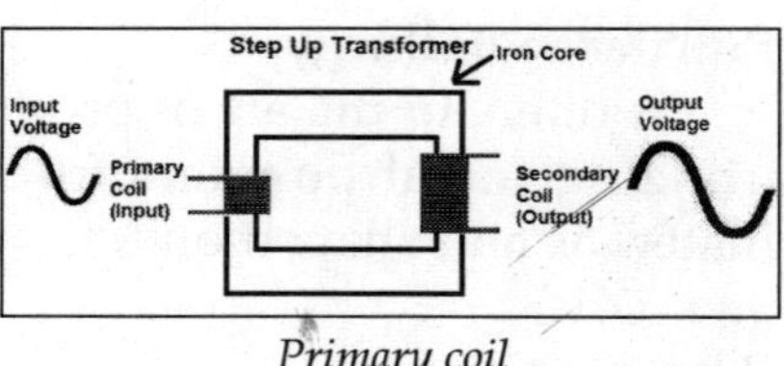

Primary coil

Primary light colours

These primary light colours include red, green or blue light.

Primary pigment

These pigments include yellow, green or magenta light.

Primary voltaic cells

These are non-rechargeable cells in which once the reactants are consumed, and electricity is generated, then no further reaction is possible.

Primary winding

It is the first coil of a transformer, the density of which determines the change to the input voltage and induces a current in the 'secondary winding'.

Principal axis

It is a reference to the line connecting center of curvature of spherical mirror with its geometric vertex.

Principle of superposition

It refers to the displacement due to two or more forces is equal to vector sum of forces.

Printed circuit

It is an electronic component designed for

interconnecting the other components, and it usually has a metallic conductor pattern on an organic insulating substrate.

Probability

It is the extent to which an event is likely to occur, measured by the ratio of the favorable cases to the whole number of cases possible.

Projectiles

It can be defined as the motion of objects given initial velocity that then move only under force of gravity.

Projector

It is a device that integrates a light source, optics system, electronics, and displays for the purpose of projecting an image from a computer or video device onto a wall or screen for large image viewing.

Projector

Proportional counter

It is referred to as a measurement device to count particles of ionizing radiation and determine their energy.

Protactinium [Pa]

Naturally occurring as a decay product of uranium, this short-lived, rare, radioactive metallic element of the actinide series with its atomic number as 91 is applied mainly in the areas of scientific research.

Proteolysis

It is the process in which the hydrolysis of proteins or

peptides into amino acids by the action of proteases takes place.

Proton

It is a subatomic particle having a mass of 1.0073 amu and a charge of +1, found in the nuclei of atoms. This subatomic particle has a positive charge that is nucleus of hydrogen atom.

Ptolemaic astronomy

Also known as the geocentric model, this theory, now discarded, that the Earth is the center of the universe and other objects orbit around it.

Pulley

It can be defined as a simple machine consisting of a wheel that rotates around a stationary axle. The outer rim of the pulley is grooved to accommodate a rope or chain.

Pulley

Pump

It is a mechanical device that moves fluid or gas by pressure or suction.

Pyramid

It refers to a polyhedron having a polygonal base and triangular sides with a common vertex.

Pyroelectricity

It is defined as the ability of certain materials to generate a temporary voltage when they are heated or cooled.

Pyrolysis

It is a thermochemical decomposition of a substance at high temperatures in the absence of oxygen.

Pyrometer

It is an instrument used to measure the infrared radiation and temperature emitted by a body or surface.

Pyrometer

Pyrophoric

This kind of substance is liable to ignite spontaneously when exposed to air.

❐

Q

Quadrature

A planet is said to be in quadrature with the Sun when the difference in ecliptic longitude is 90°.

Quantised

It is a quantity that cannot be divided into smaller increments forever, for which there exists a minimum, quantum increment.

Quanglement

This form of quantum superposition, also known as quantum entanglement, occurs when particles such as photons, electrons, molecules as large as buckyballs, and even small diamonds interact physically and then become separated.

Quantization

This phenomenon aims at explaining a classical understanding of physical phenomena in terms of a newer understanding known as "quantum mechanics".

Quantum

It is the smallest quantity of some physical property that a system can possess according to the quantum theory.

Quantum chaos

It refers to a branch of physics which studies how chaotic classical systems can be described in terms of quantum theory.

Quantum chemistry

It is a branch of theoretical chemistry concerned with quantum mechanics and quantum field theory to provide an explanation of problems in chemistry.

Quantum computing

It is defined as a method of computing, based on quantum physics, which uses the ability of particles such as electrons to exist in more than one state at the same time.

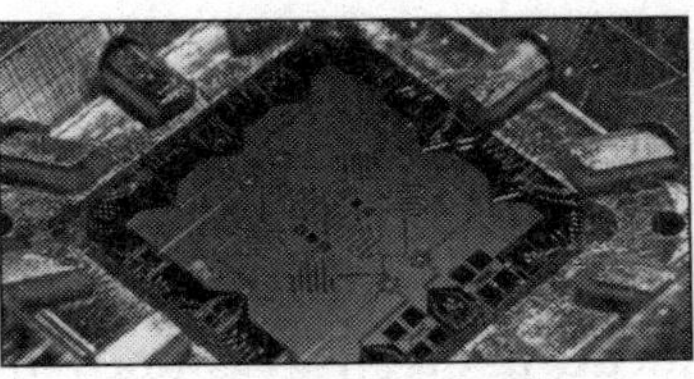

Quantum computing

Quantum dot

It is referred to as a semiconductor whose excitons are confined in all three spatial dimensions.

Quantum electrodynamics

Abbreviated as QED, it is essentially the theory of how light interacts with matter. It deals with the interactions between electrons, positrons (antielectrons) and photons.

Quantum electronics

It refers to the area of physics dealing with the effects of quantum mechanics on the behavior of electrons in matter, and their interactions with photons.

Quantum gravity

It is a proposed theory that unifies relativity with quantum mechanics under one single framework.

Quantum jump

It refers to an abrupt alteration from one energy level to another, such as the transition of an electron, atom, or molecule from one quantum state to another, with the absorption or emission of a quantum.

Quantum mechanics

It is the mathematical method of treating the motion and interaction of particles on the basis of quantum theory, assuming that the energy of small particles is not infinitely divisible.

Quantum model of atom

It can be defined as an atomic model in which only probability of locating electron is known.

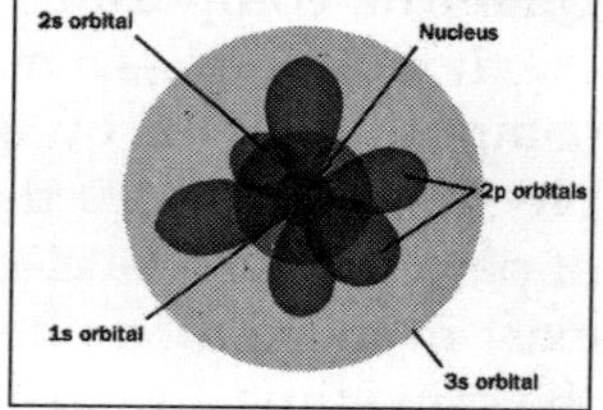

Quantum model of atom

Quantum numbers

These numbers describe the energies of electrons in atoms in the dynamics of the quantum system.

Quantum optics

It is a field of research in physics, dealing with the application of quantum mechanics to phenomena involving light and its interactions with matter.

Quantum phase transition

Abbreviated as QPT, it is a phase transition between different quantum phases (phases of matter at zero temperature).

Quantum simulation

It is the mathematical modelling of systems of large number of molecules by computer studies of relatively small clusters.

Quantum spin liquid

It is defined as a solid in which small magnetic moments have a fluctuating random orientation, even at low temperature.

Quantum state

It refers to a state of a quantized system defined by a set of quantum numbers.

Quantum teleportation

It is referred to as a technique used to transfer quantum information from one quantum system to another.

Quantum theory

Based on the concept of quantum mechanics, it is a theory of matter and energy explaining how energy can only exist at certain levels.

Quantum well

It is a potential well that confines particles, which were originally free to move in three dimensions, to two dimensions, forcing them to occupy a planar region.

Quantum wire

It is a nano-structure proportioned like a wire so that electron behavior is strongly constrained by quantum mechanical effects in two dimensions.

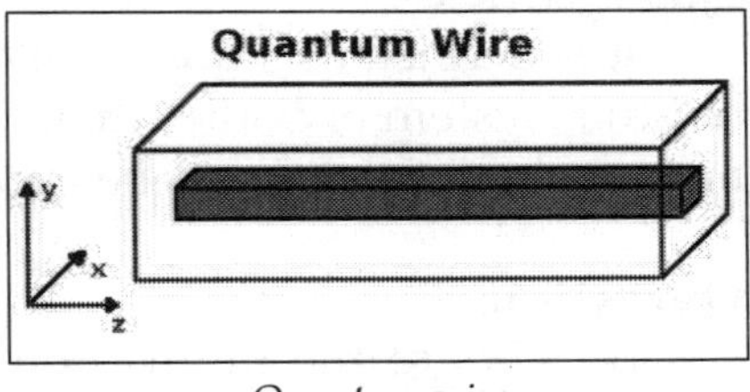

Quantum wire

Quark

It can be defined as the basic building block of protons, neutrons, other baryons, and mesons.

Quark model

It is a model in which all particles that interact via the strong interaction are composed of two or three quarks.

Quartz

Found in most rocks, this hard, glossy, abundant, white mineral comprising silicon dioxide is used in ceramics, cements, etc.

Quartz clock

It is a kind of clock that uses an electronic oscillator that is regulated by a quartz crystal to keep time.

Quasars

It is an extragalactic object, starlike in appearance, that is among the most luminous and thought to be the most distant objects in the universe.

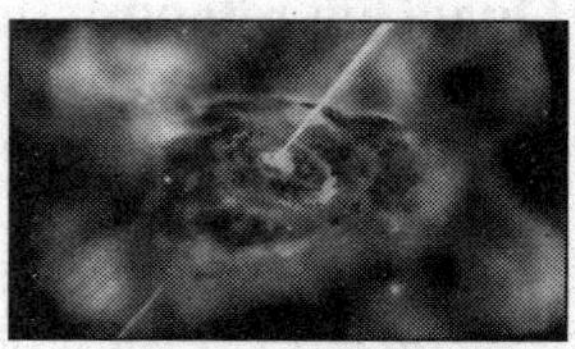

Quasars

Quasicrystal

It is an accumulation of molecules (solid material) that is crystal-like in certain properties (made of repeating structural units) but does not have a consistent spatial periodicity.

Quasiparticle

It is defined as a quantum of energy in a crystal lattice or other system of bodies that has momentum and position and can in some respects be regarded as a particle.

Quenching

It refers to the rapid cooling of heated metal for the purpose of imparting certain properties, especially hardness.

R

Racemic mixture

Also called racemate, this mixture consists of equal amounts of left and right-handed enantiomers of a chiral substance.

Radar

This electronic instrument is based on the principle that ultra-high frequency radio waves travel at a precise speed and are reflected from objects they strike. It is used to determine an object's direction and distance.

Radar

Radial field

In this particular field, the field lines diverge radially outward from a point source or converge radially inwards towards a point source.

Radiant energy

It is defined as any energy that flows outward or radiates in all directions from a source, with characteristics of both particle motion and wave motion.

Radiation

It refers to the emission of high energy particles or electromagnetic rays emitted during the nuclear decay processes.

Radiation damage

It is the damage caused by the removal of atoms from a solid material when elementary particles, such as those associated with cosmic rays or radioactivity, collide with it.

Radiationless decay

It is the decay in which electromagnetic radiation is not emitted and there is a transition of a molecule from an excited state to a lower energy state.

Radiation pressure

It is the amount of pressure exerted upon any surface exposed to electromagnetic radiation.

Radiation temperature

It is defined as the temperature that a blackbody of similar dimensions would have that radiated the same intensity at the same frequency.

Radiative collision

It is explained as a phenomenon wherein a part of the kinetic energy of the particles is converted into electromagnetic radiation, when there is a collision between two charged particles.

Radical

Generally a highly reactive species, it is an atom or group of atoms consisting of one or more unpaired electrons.

Radio

It refers to a device that allows for the transmission of sound or other signals by modulation of electromagnetic waves, and can capture (receive) the signal sent over radio waves and render the modulated signal as sound.

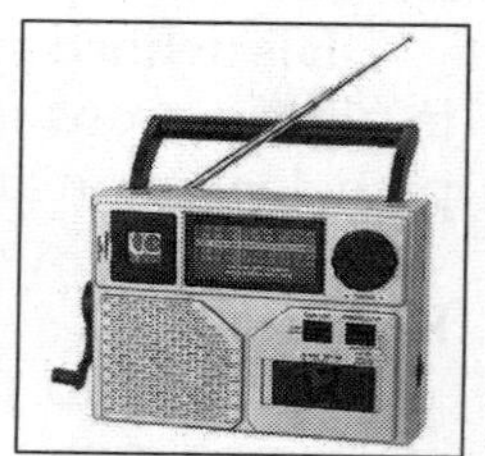

Radio

Radioactive dating

It is a technique of dating ancient objects by ascertaining the ratio of amounts of mother and daughter nuclides present in an object.

Radioactive decay

It can be referred to as a spontaneous change of unstable nuclei into other nuclei.

Radioactive materials

It can be defined as the materials that undergo radioactive decay.

Radioactive materials

Radioactive series

It refers to a chained series of nuclides, each of which changes by radioactive decay into the next until the resultant is a stable nuclide. The first member of the series is the parent, the intermediate members are daughters, and the final member is the end product.

Radioactive waste

It is defined as any waste that emits energy as rays, waves, or streams of energetic particles. Radioactive materials are often mixed with hazardous waste, usually from nuclear reactors, research institutions, etc.

Radioactivity

It is the spontaneous disintegration of atomic nuclei leading to the emission of ionising radiation or particles.

Radio astronomy

It is the study of electromagnetic radiation from outside the earth's atmosphere.

Radiobiology

It is a branch of biology which deals with the interaction

of biological systems and radiant energy or radioactive materials.

Radiochemistry

It is the chemistry that deals with radioactive substances.

Radio galaxies

These are galaxies that show exceptionally strong radio emission, too intense to be produced by the normal processes of starbirth and stardeath.

Radiogenic nuclide

It is a nuclide is one that is produced by a process of radioactive decay.

Radiography

It is the process of making radiographs on a radiosensitive surface by radiation other than visible light, and the science of analyzing them.

Radioisotopes

Produced naturally and artificially, these are atomic particles which decay by natural radioactivity.

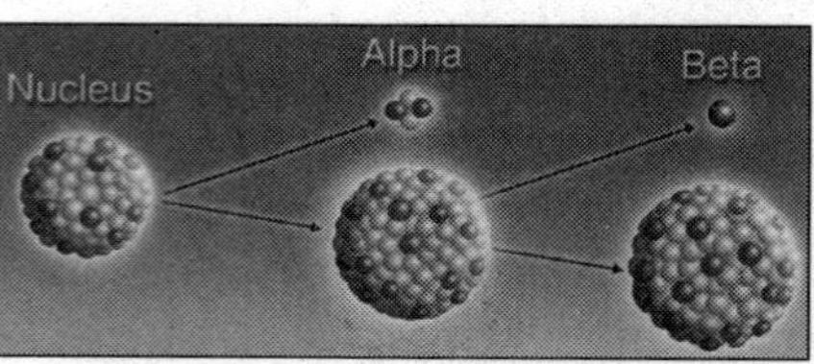

Radioisotopes

Radiology

It is the science dealing with X-rays and other high-energy radiation, especially the use of such radiation for the diagnosis and treatment of disease.

Radiolysis

It is the process in which the molecular disintegration of a substance by radiation takes place, resulting in the change in chemical compounds.

Radionuclide

It is an unstable atom, which is naturally occurring and synthetically made, and these elements emit atomic energy generally in the form of alpha and beta rays, like uranium, radon and radium.

Radiosonde

It is a device attached to a weather balloon that transmits pressure, humidity, temperature and winds as it ascends.

Radiosonde

Radio sources

These are objects in outer space that emit strong radio waves.

Radio telescope

It is an instrument used to collect radio waves emitted by celestial bodies, and it is generally by means of a large parabolic antenna (dish).

Radiotherapy

Also called radiation therapy or irradiation, it is the careful use of various forms of radiation to treat cancer and other diseases.

Radio transmission

It is defined as the wireless transmission of electromagnetic waves in the frequency range of 10 kilohertz to 300,000 megahertz.

Radiotransparent

A radiotransparent structure shows up black on X-rays.

Radium [Ra]

Naturally found in minute amounts in uranium ores, it is a rare, white, strongly oxidising, radioactive metallic element of the alkaline earth series with its atomic number as 88.

Radon [Rn]

Found as a decay product of uranium, this rare, radioactive, colourless, odourless, gaseous element belonging to the noble gas series, with its atomic number as 86, is used in the medical and scientific fields.

Rainbow

It is a luminous arc featuring all colours of the visible light spectrum (red, orange, yellow, green, blue, indigo, and violet), which is produced by refraction, total reflection, and the dispersion of light.

Rainbow

Range of projectile

It is the horizontal distance between launch point of projectile and where it returns to launch height.

Raoult's law

This law states that the vapour pressure of a solvent in an ideal solution decreases as its mole fraction decreases.

Rarefaction

It is the reduction of a medium's density, or the opposite of compression due to the action of the molecules moving apart.

Ray model of light

It can be defined as the light, which may be represented by straight line along the direction of motion.

Ray

It is a beam of light or radiation.

Ray optics

It means the study of light using ray model.

Rayleigh criterion

It can be referred to as – two optical images are separable if central bright spot of one image falls on first dark band of second.

Real gas

It is opposed to an ideal gas, and is therefore known as a non-ideal gas. Usually, these gases at sufficiently high pressures and low temperatures are non-ideal.

Real image

It is a kind of optical image at which rays from an object converge.

Recalescence

It implies an increase in temperature that occurs after undercooling, because the rate of liberation of heat during transformation of a material exceeds the rate of dissipation of heat.

Receiver

It is a device that detects electromagnetic waves.

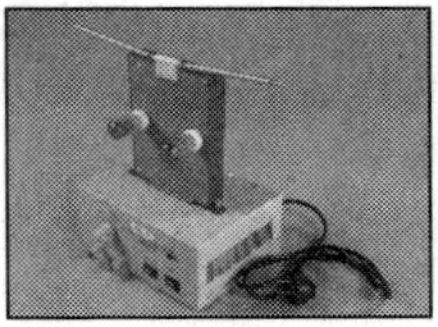

Receiver

Rectification

It is the act of converting an AC voltage source into DC voltage.

Rectifier

It is a self-contained unit for converting a.c. mains to d.c. for charging a battery and supplying the load.

Reference level

It can be defined as the level or location at which potential energy is chosen to be zero.

Red dwarf

It is known as a smaller star with a low mass, cooler, and less luminous than the sun.

Red giant

It is known as a very large, distended, and relatively cool star which is in the final stages of its life.

Reference point

It is referred to as zero location in a coordinate system or frame of reference.

Reflection

It is the (i) act of reflecting or the state of being reflected such as an image; (ii) property of a propagated wave being thrown back from a surface (such as a mirror).

Refraction

It can be defined as the change in direction of light ray when passing from one medium to another.

Refractive index

It implies the ratio of speed of light in vacuum to that in the medium.

Refractivity

It is explained as a measure of the speed of light in that substance.

Refractometer

This laboratory or field device is used mainly for the measurement of an index of refraction.

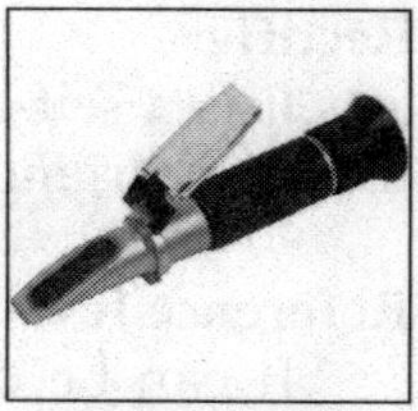

Refractometer

Refrigeration

It is mainly the phenomenon in which heat is removed

from an enclosed space, or from a substance, and is moved to a place where it is unobjectionable.

Relative density

It is the ratio of the density of a substance to the density of a standard.

Relative molecular mass

It is the sum of all the relative atomic masses of the constituent atoms of a molecule.

Remote sensing

This is the practice of acquiring and using data from satellites and aerial photography to infer or measure land cover/use.

Remote sensing

Renewable energy sources

These sources of energy can be naturally replenished and are derived from natural resources such as sunlight, wind, rain, etc.

Renormalization

It is a method used in quantum mechanics in which unwanted infinities are removed from the solutions of equations by redefining parameter.

Reptation

It is a particular thermal motion of very long linear macromolecules (polymer chains) in the melts and concentrated solutions of polymers.

Resistance

It is referred to as the ratio of potential difference across a device to the current through it.

Resistance force

It is the force that is exerted by a machine.

Resistor

It is a kind of device designed to have a specific resistance.

Resolution

It is a phenomenon by which a racemic mixture is separated into its two constituent enantiomorphs.

Resonance

It is the concept in which two or more conventional formulas form the same arrangement of atoms needed for describing the bonding in a molecule.

Responding variable

It can be defined as the variable that changes as a result of change in manipulated variable.

Rest energy

It means the energy due to mass of object ($E = mc^2$).

Resultant

It is the vector sum of two or more vectors.

Retina

It is the thin layer of cells at the back of the eyeball where light is converted into neural signals sent to the brain.

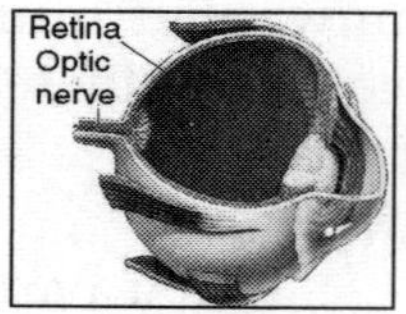

Retina

Retrograde motion

It is explained as the orbital or rotational movement in the opposite sense to that of Earth's motion.

Retrorocket

It is a type of rocket engine that gives thrust in a direction opposite to the direction of the object's motion.

Reverberatory furnace

It is a metallurgical or process furnace that isolates the material being processed from contact with the fuel, but not from contact with combustion gases.

Reverse osmosis

In this process, pure water is produced by forcing solvent molecules to flow through a semi-permeable membrane from a concentrated solution into a dilute solution by the application of greater hydrostatic pressure.

Reversible process

In this process, a system can be made to go through the same steps in the reverse order.

Rheopexy

It is a rare property of some non-Newtonian fluids exhibited by some slow-gelling, thixotropic sols of gelling more rapidly when subjected to shaking gently.

Rheostat

It is an electrical appliance used to raise or lower the resistance of a circuit and correspondingly to decrease or increase the current flowing.

Rheostat

Richter scale

It refers to a measure of the total amount of energy released during an earthquake, which runs from 1 to 10 on a logarithmic scale.

Right-hand rules

It is primarily used to find force on current or moving particle in magnetic field.

Robotics

It is defined as the engineering science and technology

of robots, and their design, manufacture, application, and structural disposition.

Rochelle salt

Also known as a potassium sodium tartrate, this double salt acts as a cathartic and is also used in Seidlitz powder.

Rocket

It is a missile or vehicle propelled by the combustion of a fuel and a contained oxygen supply. The forward thrust of a rocket results when exhaust products are ejected from the tail.

Rocket

Rod

It is a light-sensitive cell of one of the two types present in large numbers in the retina of the eye, and it is responsible mainly for monochrome vision in poor light.

Roentgenium [Rg]

Produced artificially, it is a radioactive transuranic element of atomic number 111.

Rose's metal

Another name for rose's alloy, this fusible alloy with a low melting point is made of bismuth, lead and tin and is mainly used as a solder.

Rotary converter

It is known as a type of electrical machine which acts as

a mechanical rectifier or inverter, which was used earlier to convert AC to DC or DC to AC power.

Rotor

It is a rotating part of a mechanical device, for example in an electric motor, generator, alternator or pump.

Rotor

Rusting

It is the formation of reddish-brown corrosion product on iron by low-temperature oxidation due to the presence of moisture.

Rutherfordium [Rf]

Produced artificially by high-energy atomic collisions, it is an unstable element with its atomic number as 104.

Rutherford's model of atom

It is a nuclear model of atom, and is essentially all masses in compact, positively-charged object at center, surrounded by electrons.

S

Sacrificial protection

It refers to a particular corrosion protection technique that utilises a metal of lower electrode potential to guard a metal of higher electrode potential.

Salinometer

It is a hydrometer for determining the salinity of a solution.

Satellite

It is defined as (i) a celestial body that orbits a planet or smaller body, such as Moon orbiting around the Earth; (ii) an object which has been placed into orbit by human endeavor and are thus called artificial satellites.

Satellite

Scalene

It usually relates to a triangle whose all the sides are unequal.

Scalar

It is referred to as a quantity, like distance, that has only a magnitude, or size.

Scanning

It is a process of causing a surface, object, or part of the body to be traversed by a detector or an electromagnetic beam.

Schematic diagram

It is the representation of electric circuit using symbols.

Schlieren photography

It is an experimental photographic technique for detecting the presence of slight density variations in fluids by virtue of refraction effects.

Schrodinger's cat

This thought experiment, conducted by Austrian physicist Erwin Schrödinger in 1935, explained the problem of the Copenhagen interpretation of quantum mechanics applied to everyday objects, resulting in a contradiction with common sense.

Scientific notation

These are the numbers expressed in this form $M*10^n$, where $1< M<10$, and n is an integer.

Scintillation

It can be defined as a flash of light, which is emitted when a substance is struck by radiation.

Scintillation counter

It is a device used to detect and measure radioactivity by detecting gamma rays, and is more sensitive than a Geiger counter.

Sclerometer

It refers to a measuring device that determines the hardness of objects by penetrating them with a stylus with a diamond point.

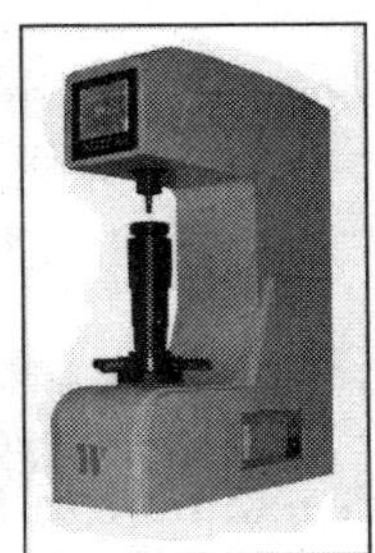

Sclerometer

Scotopic vision

It is defined as the vision under relatively low light levels when the visual response is primarily controlled by the rods.

Screw

It refers to a threaded cylindrical pin or rod with a head at one end, used to hold parts together.

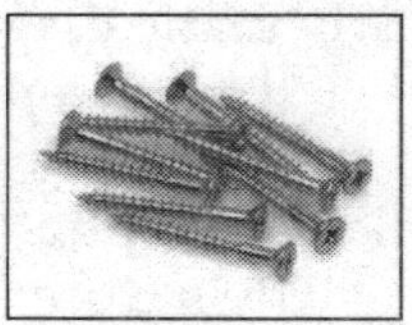

Screw

Seaborgium [Sg]

Produced artificially by high-energy atomic collisions, it is a very unstable, transuranic element of atomic number 106.

Search coil

It is a flat coil of insulated wire linked to a galvanometer, and is used for searching the strength of a magnetic field from the current induced in the coil when it is quickly turned over.

Searle's bar method

This method is an experimental procedure to measure thermal conductivity of material.

Second [symbol: s]

It is the SI unit of time, where there are 60 seconds in a minute.

Second law of thermodynamics

It is the heat flow only from the region of high temperature to the region of lower temperature.

Secondary cell

It is a rechargeable voltaic cell, in which original reactants can be regenerated by reversing the direction of the electric current.

Secondary coil

It can be referred to as a transformer coil in which varying EMF is induced.

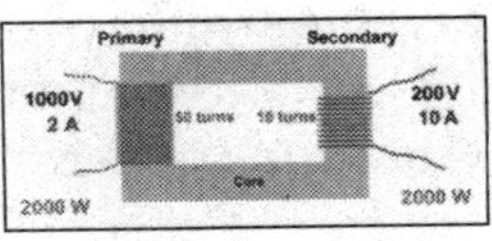

Secondary coil

Secondary emission

It is a process in which primary incident particles of sufficient energy, when hitting a surface or passing through some material, induce the emission of secondary particles.

Secondary light colours

The secondary light colours include yellow, cyan or magenta light.

Secondary pigment

The secondary pigments include red, green or blue pigment.

Secondary winding

It is a winding which is not connected to the power source, but which carries current induced in it through its magnetic linkage with the primary winding.

Second-order reaction

In this reaction, the reaction rate is proportional to the concentration of each of the two reacting molecules or chemical species.

Sedimentation

It is a method in which heavier, suspended matter is separated from a liquid solution, and is used for measuring the size of large molecules.

Seismic waves

These are waves that transmit the energy released and generated by energy related because of displacement of the Earth or any movement of the Earth's crust.

Seismograph

It is a scientific instrument that detects and records vibrations or seismic waves produced by earthquakes.

Seismology

It is defined as the branch of science concerned with earthquakes and related phenomena.

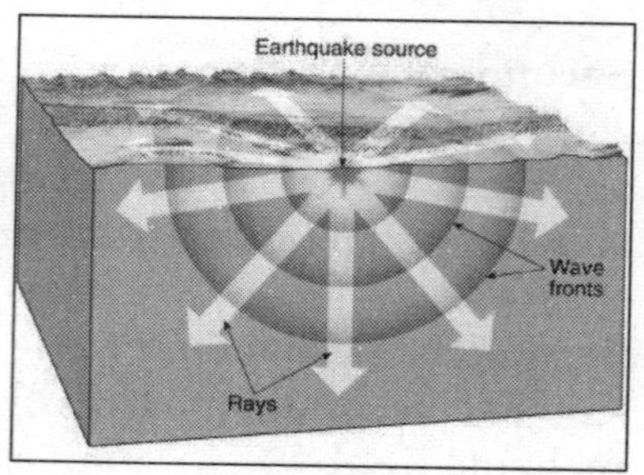

Seismology

Selenium cell

This solar cell is a photoelectric device which consists of a strip of selenium and generates electric current according to the intensity of light.

Selenology

It is the scientific study of the Moon's movements in the heavens and the kinetic influences it has upon and it receives from other astronomical bodies.

Self-exciting generator

It is a kind of excitation of generators where the magnetic field of the main poles is excited by a current supplied to the windings of the main poles from the armature winding.

Self-organisation

It is the ability of a system to create a well-defined molecular entity spontaneously by organising from components in a particular condition.

Self-inductance

It can be defined as the induced EMF produced in coil by changing current.

Semiconductor

It is a substance (germanium, silicon, etc.) with electrical properties intermediate between a good conductor and a good insulator, and as the temperature rises, its conductivity increases.

Semiconductor laser

It refers to a light-emitting diode designed to use stimulated emission to form a coherent light output.

Semimetal

These substances have properties of both metals and non-metals, such as antimony, cobalt, zinc, etc.

Semipermeable membrane

It is a thin partition between two solutions through which certain molecules (based on size and charge) can pass but others cannot.

Series circuit

It is a circuit in which electrical current flows through each component, one after another.

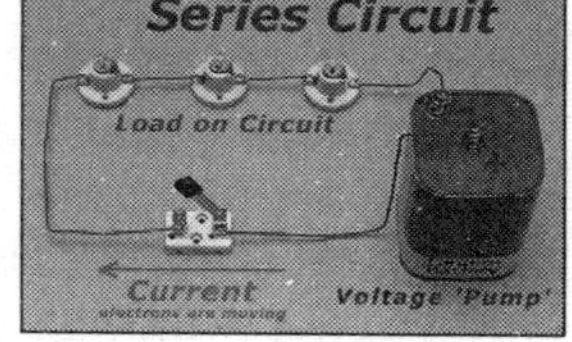

Series circuit

Series connection

It refers to an arrangement of electrical devices so that there is only one path through which current can flow.

Sextant

It is a navigational device for obtaining angular distances between objects so as to determine latitude and longitude.

Shadow

It is an area where direct light from a light source cannot reach due to obstruction by an object.

Sherardizing

It is a cementation process where zinc dust is heated to a temperature near its molten point and is brought into intimate contact with the steel surface to form an iron and zinc coating on the steel by diffusion.

Shock wave

It is a sudden alteration of pressure in a narrow region travelling through a liquid or gas at a velocity greater than that of sound.

Short circuit

It can be referred to as a low resistance connection between two points, which is often accidental.

Short-sightedness

Another name for myopia, it is an eyesight abnormality resulting from the eye's faulty refractive ability, where distant objects appear blurred.

Shunt

It is an electrical conductor joining two points of a circuit, through which more or less of a current may be diverted.

Shunt

Sidereal period

It is the time taken by a planet or satellite to describe a complete orbit, referred to the stars.

Signal

It is an electrical or electromagnetic action, normally a voltage that is a function of time that conveys the information of the radio or TV program or of communication.

Significant digit

These are the reliable digits reported in a measurement.

Silicon chip

It refers to an electronic device consisting of a small crystal of a silicon semiconductor designed to process a number of electronic functions in an integrated circuit.

Silicon chip

Simple harmonic motion

It is a motion caused by linear restoring that has a period independent of amplitude of motion.

Simple machine

It is a machine consisting of only one lever, inclined plane, wedge, screw, pulley, or wheel and axle.

Sine

It is the ratio of the opposite side and the hypotenuse.

Sine wave

It is a waveform corresponding to a single-frequency periodic oscillation that can be mathematically represented as a function of amplitude versus angle in which the value of the curve at any point is equal to the sine of that angle.

Sintering

It is the process of combining/fusing metals, (usually with pressure and temperature) by exposing them to a temperature just below their melting point.

SI unit

Known as Standard International unit, it is a specific system of metric units for measuring physical quantities such as length, volume, temperature, etc.

Skyrmion

It is a mathematical model used to model baryons (a subatomic particle).

Sliding friction

It is the force between two surfaces in relative motion.

Slope

It is the ratio of the vertical separation, or rise to the horizontal separation, or run.

Smoke

It is explained as the visible vapour/vapour, gases, and fine particles given off by burning or smoldering material.

Smelting

It is a kind of extractive metallurgical operation, which is used to produce a metal after it is separated by fusion from its ores.

Soap

Prepared from fats and sodium hydroxide, this substance can mix with both water and oil, and is typically used as a cleansing agent.

Soap

Sodium-sulphur cell

It is a kind of secondary cell that has molten electrodes of sodium and sulphur divided by a solid electrolyte made of beta alumina.

Sodium-vapour lamp

It refers to a gas discharge lamp which uses sodium in an excited state to produce artificial light.

Soft iron

It is defined as a particular type of iron that has a low carbon content and is easily magnetized and demagnetized.

Soft matter

It is a subfield of condensed matter consisting of a variety of physical states that are easily deformed by thermal stresses or thermal fluctuations.

Soft radiation

It is referred to as high-energy electromagnetic radiation, typically high energy X-rays or gamma rays.

Software

It signifies any program that can be run and stored on a computer for specific uses, including communications, data processing, entertainment, and management tools.

Software

Soft water

This form of water does not contain mineral salts (calcium or magnesium), and allows the formation of lather with soap.

Sol

It is a fluid suspension of a colloidal solid in a liquid.

Solar cell

It is explained as a device made of silicon and semiconductor materials, producing electricity when exposed to sunlight.

Solar energy

It is the radiant energy from the Sun that influences Earth's climate and weather and sustains life. It includes visible light and several non-visible frequencies such as ultraviolet light.

Solar heating

It refers to the technologies or systems that take advantage of the heat energy coming from the sun. Solar thermal collectors are used in solar hot water systems and photovoltaic collectors are used in solar electric systems.

Solar system

It is defined as a system that is made of the Sun and other celestial bodies within its gravitational influence, including planets, asteroids, satellites, comets, and meteors.

Solar system

Solar wind

It is the particle flux related to the interplanetary magnetic field. It is composed primarily of electrons and protons, which is expelled continuously from the Sun toward space.

Solder

This low-melting, fusible metal alloy is used in joining metallic surfaces (soldering), electronics, plumbing, etc.

Solid

It is a state of matter with fixed volume and shape.

Solid solution

It is a crystalline phase of solution that is homogeneous but has several different chemical components, whose molecules are randomly distributed on the points of the space lattice.

Solid-state physics

It is the study of rigid matter, or solids, through methods such as quantum mechanics, crystallography, electromagnetism, and metallurgy. It is the largest branch of condensed matter physics.

Solubility

It is the amount of a substance that can dissolve in a particular solvent.

Solubility product

It is a kind of dynamic equilibrium for a reaction, where a solid ionic compound dissolves to yield its ions in a saturated solution.

Solute

It is the dispersed or dissolved phase of a solution.

Solution

It is a homogeneous mixture of two or more substances.

Solvation

In this process, the solvent molecules surround and interact with solute molecules.

Solvent

It is the dispersing medium of a solution.

Sonic boom

It is a loud explosive noise caused by the shock wave from an aircraft traveling faster than the speed of sound.

Sonic boom

Sonochemistry

This branch of chemistry is related to the understanding of the effect of ultrasonic energy (sonic waves and wave properties) on chemical systems.

Sonometer

It is an apparatus by which the transverse vibrations of strings and sensitivity of hearing can be studied.

Sorption

It is the accumulation of molecules of a substance by another in a different phase.

Sorption pump

It is a vacuum pump that creates a vacuum by adsorbing molecules on a very porous material like molecular sieve.

Sorption pump

Sound

It includes vibrations that travel through the air or another medium and can be heard when they reach a person's or animal's ear.

Sound level

It is the quantity measuring logarithm of sound intensity in decibels.

Spark

It can be defined as (i) a small particle of glowing matter, either molten or on fire; (ii) a short or small burst of electrical discharge.

Spark chamber

It is a device used to detect the path of charged subatomic particles by a spark that jumps along the path of ionization created in a gas.

Specific gravity

It can be defined as the ratio of the density of a substance to the density of reference substance.

Specific heat

It is the thermal energy that needs to change temperature of unit mass of substance to one Kelvin.

Spectrochemical series

It is an arrangement of ligands in order of increasing ligand field strength.

Spectrometer

It is an instrument used for recording and measuring spectra (wavelengths of light).

Spectroscope

It is an instrument used for producing and recording spectra by splitting it up into its component colours.

Spectroscope

Spectroscopy

It is explained as the technique of observing the spectra of visible light from an object to determine its composition, temperature, density, and speed.

Spectrum

It is a collection of wavelengths in an electromagnetic spectrum.

Speed

It is a ratio of distance travelled to time interval.

Speed of light

It implies the speed at which light is propagated through some medium under specified conditions. The speed of light in vacuum is 2.9979458 * 10^8 m/s.

Speed of sound

It implies the speed at which sound is propagated

through some medium under specified conditions. The speed of sound in still air at 0 degrees Celsius is 331 m/s.

Spherical aberration

It refers to the inability of spherical mirror to focus all parallel rays to a single point.

Spherometer

It is a measuring device for determining the curvature of a surface.

Spherometer

Spiegel

It is a lustrous, crystalline pig iron which has large quantities of manganese and is used as a deoxidising agent and in steel manufacturing.

Spin glass

It is a magnet with frustrated interactions, augmented by stochastic disorder, where usually ferromagnetic and antiferromagnetic bonds are randomly distributed.

Spontaneous emission

It refers to the relaxation of an excited state to a ground state with the emission of a photon.

Spring balance

It is an apparatus for weighing articles by noting the compression of a helical spring.

Sputtering

In this process, there is an accumulation of metal on a surface by using fast ions to eject particles of it from a target. It is used for thin-film deposition, etching, etc.

Stainless steel

Also called inox steel, this form of steel consists of

chromium, which makes it resistant to staining, tarnishing and corrosion.

Standard electrode

It is a kind of half-cell, in which the oxidized and reduced forms of a species are present at unit activity.

Standard conditions

Abbreviated as E° or Eo, it is the measure of individual potential of a reversible electrode under standard conditions.

Standing wave

Also known as stationary wave, it is a wave with stationary nodes, which remains in a constant position.

Star

It is explained as a luminous celestial body, made up of plasma (particularly hydrogen and helium) and having a spherical shape.

Star

Star cluster

It is a group of stars, bound together by their mutual gravity, occupying a certain volume of space and showing common proper motion.

Starquake

It is a type of quake, which is the result when the surface of a planet, moon, or star begins to "shake" having a noticeable feel.

Static electricity

It is a kind of electrical charge that builds up due to friction between two dissimilar materials. Friction removes some electrons from one object and deposits them on the other.

Static friction

It can be defined as a kind of force that opposes the start of motion between two surfaces.

Statistical mechanics

It is the application of probability theory to the study of the thermodynamic behaviour of systems composed of a large number of particles.

Stator

It is the part of a motor, generator or alternator that does not rotate. In permanent magnet alternators it holds the coils and laminates.

Steam distillation

It is a kind of separation process of a liquid in a current of steam, which is used to separate botanical matter from essential oils that are immiscible with water.

Steam engine

It is an engine in which a portion of the heat energy of the fuel is conveyed to the cylinder by means of steam, which expands behind the piston and drives it forward.

Steam engine

Steam point

It is the temperature at which water vapour condenses at a pressure of one atmosphere, and is illustrated by 100°C and 212°F.

Steel

Consisting mainly of iron and carbon, this hard, strong, grey-coloured alloy is used mainly as a structural and fabricating material, such as in construction, etc.

Stellar evolution

It refers to the several phases in the lifetime of a star, from its formation out of gas and dust, to the time after its nuclear fuel is exhausted.

Stellar wind

It is explained as a torrent of charged atomic particles emanating from stars, wherein there is a release of gas from a star's surface.

Step-down transformer

It is a kind of transformer with output voltage smaller than input voltage.

Step-down transformer

Step-up transformer

It is a kind of transformer with output voltage larger than input voltage.

Stereochemistry

This branch of chemistry is related to the three-dimensional spatial arrangements of atoms within molecules, and its effects on the properties of molecules.

Stimulated emission

It is an emission of photon from an excited atom caused by the impact of a photon of the same energy.

Stoichiometry

It is a description of the quantitative relationships among the elements and compounds as they undergo chemical changes.

Strain gauge

It is an instrument that measures the strain in a structural element by measuring changes in electrical resistance of a sensor attached to the element under scrutiny.

Stratosphere

It is the zone in the atmosphere extending from the tropopause to about 50 km (30 mi) above the earth's surface, where temperatures are stable or rise slightly with altitude, and it also has very little water vapor but is rich in ozone.

Stripping reaction

It is a nuclear reaction in which part of the incident nucleus combines with the target nucleus, and the remainder proceeds with most of its original momentum in almost its original direction.

Stroboscope

It is a device used to measure motion by using an adjustable flashing light to make moving devices appear to be stationary.

Strong nuclear force

It is referred to as a force of very short range that holds neutrons and protons in nucleus together.

Sublimation

It is the direct vapourisation of a solid by heating without becoming liquid.

Sun

It is the parent star situated at the center of the Solar System. The structure of Sun's interior is the result of the hydrostatic equilibrium between gravity and the pressure of the gas. Its interior consists of three shells: the core, radiative region, and convective region.

Sun

Sunspots

These are dark regions on the Sun which are the centers of large vortices and possess powerful magnetic fields. It takes a roughly 11-year sunspot cycle, which causes slight differences in the amount of energy that the sun emits.

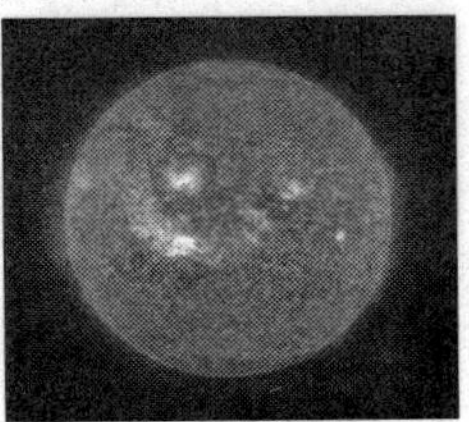

Sunspots

Superconductor

It refers to a kind of electrical conductor that has no resistance and has low temperatures.

Superconductivity

It is an illustration of a property of a material characterized by zero electric resistivity and, ideally, zero permeability. It is usually exhibited by certain materials at extremely low temperatures.

Supercooling

Another name for undercooling, it is lowering the temperature of a liquid or a gas below its freezing point, without actually obtaining the transformation.

Superfluidity

It is a state of matter in which the matter behaves like a fluid without viscosity and with infinite thermal conductivity.

Supergiant

It is primarily a dying star of extremely high luminosity and relatively cool surface temperature, whose diameter is over 100 times that of the Sun.

Superheating

Sometimes called boiling delay, it is the process in which a liquid is heated to a temperature higher than its boiling point without its vapourisation.

Supernova

It is a huge stellar explosion involving the destruction of a massive star and resulting in a spontaneous and tremendous illumination.

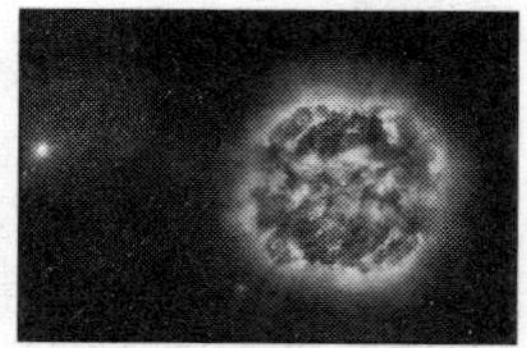

Supernova

Superplasticity

It refers to the ability of certain metals to develop extremely high tensile elongations at elevated temperatures and under controlled rates of deformation.

Supersaturation

It is a solution consisting of a higher than saturation concentration of solute, which is usually not possible.

Surface wave

It is a wave on surface of liquid with characteristics of both longitudinal and transverse waves.

Surfactant

Functioning as a wetting agent, this substance reduces the surface tension of a liquid in which the dissolution takes place.

Suspension

It is a heterogeneous mixture in which solid particles settle out of fluid-like phase.

Symmetry

It means a property that is now charged when operation or reference frame is charged.

Synchrotron

It is a kind of device to accelerate particles in which particles move in circular path.

Synthetic

It is a compound or product prepared artificially by chemical reactions.

Synthetic metal

It is a material that is not a metal but has free electrons that can contribute to electrical conductivity.

Synthetic metal

System

It is a defined collection of objects.

T

Tachometer

It refers to a device used to indicate the speed of the engine in rpm (revolutions or cycler per minute).

Tachometer

Tachyons

These are hypothesized subatomic particles which always travel at speeds in excess of the speed of light.

Tandem generator

It is a kind of particle generator, essentially consisting of a Van de Graaff generator that maintains one electrode at a high positive potential.

Tangent

It is the ratio of the opposite side and the adjacent side.

Tangent galvanometer

It is an early measuring instrument consisting of a coil of insulated copper wire wound on a circular non-magnetic frame and was used for small electric currents, which was based on the principle of the tangent law of magnetism.

Technetium [Tc]

Derived synthetically as one of the fission products of

uranium, it is a crystalline, radioactive metallic element of atomic number 43.

Tektite

It is a small, glassy material formed by the impact of a large body, usually a meteor or asteroid. Tektites are commonly found at the sites of meteor craters.

Telecommunications

It is the transmission and reception of information-bearing electrical signals between remote systems.

Telephoto lens

It refers to a camera lens that moves past unwanted foreground images, focusing on background imagery, and shortening the distances between them.

Telescope

It is a monocular optical instrument possessing magnification for observing distant objects, especially in astronomy.

Television

It is defined as the transmission of pictures and sound by radio frequency or cable for public reception.

Television

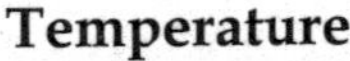

Temperature

It is a measure of the intensity of heat (the hotness or coldness) of a substance.

Tempering

It is a heat treatment method for metals, alloys and glass to improve their hardness and elasticity.

Temporary hardness

Commonly called carbonate hardness, it refers to the

hardness in water because of the presence of calcium and magnesium carbonates and bicarbonates which can be removed by heating.

Temporary magnet

It acts as a magnet only as long as it is in the magnetic field produced by a permanent magnet or an electric current.

Tensile strength

It is the longitudinal stress required to break a specimen of prescribed dimension divided by the original cross-sectional area at the point of rupture.

Tensimeter

It is a manometer for measuring and determining vapor pressure.

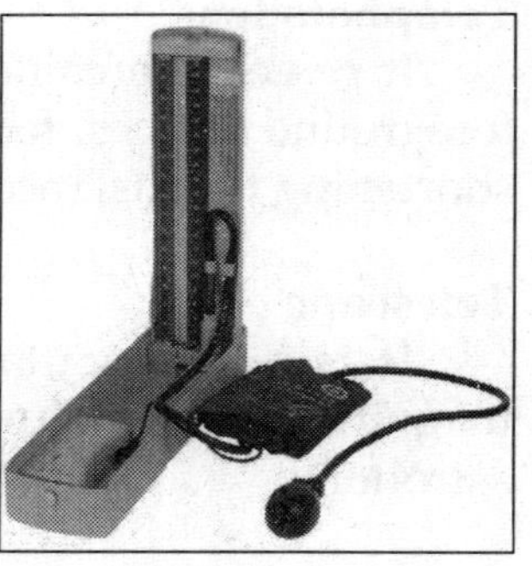

Tensimeter

Tensiometer

It is a device for measuring soil moisture, consisting of a buried tube of water that develops a partial vacuum as surrounding soil dries out.

Terminal

It is the (i) parts of a battery to which the external electric circuit is connected; (ii) metal wire termination devices designed to handle one or more conductors, and to be attached to a board, bus, or block with mechanical fasteners.

Terminal velocity

It is the velocity of falling object reached when force of air resistance equals weight.

Terminator

It is an instrument that provides electrical resistance at the end of a transmission line.

Tertiary colours

Also called intermediate colours, these are a mixture of primary and secondary colours. These colours are created by mixing a primary and secondary colour. Specifically, there are six tertiary colours: red-orange, red-violet, yellow-orange, yellow-green, blue-green and blue-violet.

Tesla coil

It is a special type of high frequency air core transformer capable of producing very high voltage AC discharges.

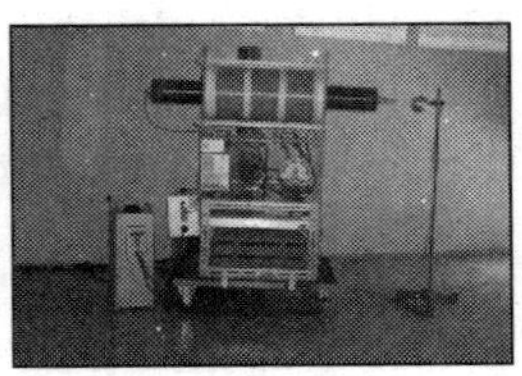

Tesla coil

Test charge

It is the charge used, in principle, to measure electric field.

Tetrahedron

It is a polyhedron composed of four triangular faces, three of which meet at each vertex.

Tetrode

It is a four-element electron tube, containing a control grid, screen grid, cathode, and plate as active elements, in addition to the filament.

Theodolite

It is an optical device which, superseding the circumferentor and graphometer, is used for general surveying purposes and by naval hydrograghers.

Theoretical physics

It is a branch of physics dealing with the theories and concepts of matter, especially at the atomic and subatomic levels.

Thermal conductivity

It is the time rate of heat flow through unit thickness of a flat slab of a homogenous material in the perpendicular direction to the slab surfaces induced by unit temperature gradient.

Thermal cracking

It refers to the decomposition by heating a substance in the presence of a catalyst and in the absence of air.

Thermal diffusion

Also known as thermodiffusion, it is a phenomenon in which a temperature gradient in a mixture of fluids gives rise to a flow of one constituent relative to the mixture as a whole.

Thermal energy

It is the internal energy, in which the sum of kinetic and potential energy of random motion of particles makes up an object.

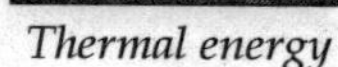

Thermal energy

Thermal equilibrium

It refers to a state in which all the parts of a system are at the same temperature, which are unchanging in time and uniform in space.

Thermal expansion

It can be an increase of length or volume of object due to change in temperature.

Thermal imaging

It is the technique of using the heat given off by an object to produce an image of it or locate it.

Thermalization

It is the process of particles reaching thermal equilibrium through mutual interaction.

Thermionics

It is the branch of science and technology that deals with thermionic emission.

Thermionic valve

It is referred to as an electron/vacuum tube consisting of a system of electrodes arranged in an evacuated glass or metal envelope.

Thermistor

It is a semiconductor which exhibits rapid and extremely large changes in resistance for relatively small alterations in temperature.

Thermochemistry

It is the branch of chemistry related to the quantities of heat generated or absorbed during chemical reactions and physical transformations.

Thermocouple

It is a pair of dissimilar conductors joined to produce a thermoelectric effect and used to accurately determine temperature.

Thermodynamics

It is the study of the energy transfers accompanying physical and chemical processes.

Thermometer

It is a device for measuring and indicating temperature.

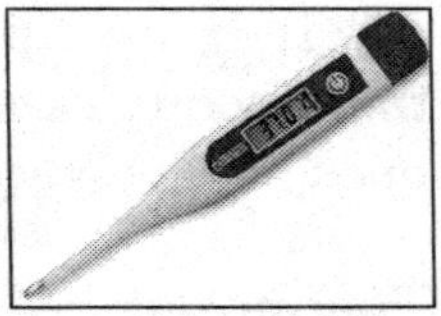

Thermometer

Thermoelectricity

It refers to the process of deriving energy from external sources (e.g., solar power, thermal energy, wind energy, salinity gradients, and kinetic energy), captured, and stored.

Thermograph

It is defined as an instrument designed to make an automatic record of temperature with time.

Thermograph

Thermography

This process measures the temperature on the skin surface to locate inflammation of muscles and soft tissues.

Thermoluminescence

It is the property of some materials that have gathered energy over a long period of becoming luminescent when pretreated and subjected to high temperatures.

Thermometer

It refers to an instrument that measures temperature or temperature gradient using a variety of different principles.

Thermonuclear reaction

It is a kind of reaction consisting of nuclear fusion.

Thermonuclear reactor

It is defined as a nuclear reactor that uses controlled nuclear fusion to generate energy.

Thermopile

It is an apparatus that consists of a number of thermocouples combined so as to multiply the effect and is used for generating electrical current.

Thermostat

It is a device that automatically regulates temperature by starting or stopping the supply of heat to maintain the temperature at a desired setting.

Thin-film interference

It means a light interference caused by reflection from both front and rear surfaces of thin layer of liquid or solid.

Thorium [Th]

Occurring naturally as thorite and monazite sands, and also as a byproduct of uranium decay, this soft, white, tetravalent, radioactive metallic element of the actinide series with its atomic number as 90 is used mainly in nuclear reactors.

Thrust

It is a reaction force described quantitatively by Newton's second and third laws. When a system expels or accelerates mass in one direction the accelerated mass will cause a proportional but opposite force on that system.

Thunderstorm

It refers to a transient, sometimes violent storm of thunder and lightning, often accompanied by rain and sometimes hail.

Thyratron

It is a special type of gas-filled triode tube designed to switch high voltage and high current in DC pulse mode.

Thyristor

It is a semiconductor bistable switch (with on and off states) that operates uni-directionally or bi-directionally.

Tides

They are an increase and decrease in sea level resulting from the moon's and, to a lesser extent, sun's gravitational pull.

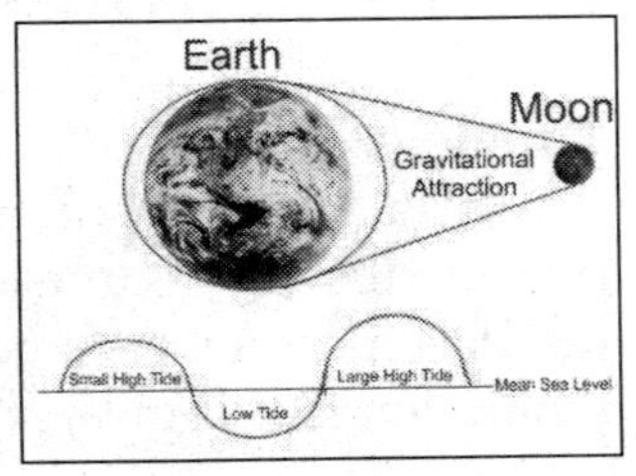

Tides

Timbre

It is a sound quality or tone colour; spectrum of sound frequencies that produce a complete wave.

Time

It refers to measuring the time or duration of an event or action or the person who performs an action in a certain period of time.

Time interval

It is a difference in time between the two clock readings.

Time travel

It usually refers to any movement through time that is not equivalent to the normal course of time, in particular a person's travel leading either to the past or faster as usual to the future.

Tokamak

It is a type of fusion reactor.

Tomography

It is an x-ray based technique used to obtain diagnostic images of a selected plane section through the human body.

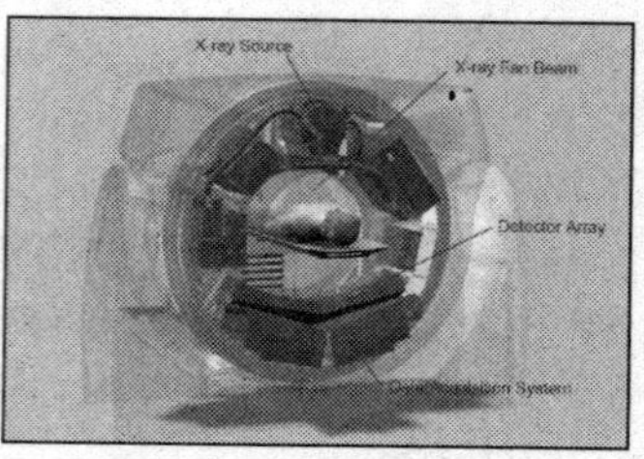

Tomography

Tone colour

It refers to timbre or tone quality.

Topology

It is a branch of mathematics concerned with those properties of geometric configurations which remain unaltered under very general kinds of elastic deformations where length, angles, and shapes are changed.

Torque

It is a product of force and the lever arm.

Torsion balance

It is a device for measuring very weak forces by their effect on a system of fine twisted wire.

Trajectory

It refers to the path followed by projectile.

Transactinide elements

Known as the super-heavy elements, these are the chemical elements with atomic numbers greater than those of the actinides.

Transducer

It is an electro-mechanical device responsible for transfiguring one form of energy to another.

Transformer

It is a device to transform energy from one electrical circuit to another by means of mutual inductance between two coils.

Transistor

It is a semiconductor device that controls large current by means of small voltage changes.

Translucent

It can be defined as a material transmitting light without distorting its path.

Transmitter

It is an electronic device which, usually with the aid of an antenna, propagates an electromagnetic signal such as radio, television, or other telecommunications.

Transmitter

Transmutation

It is a nuclear change from one element to another.

Transparent

It is a material transmitting light without distorting directions of waves.

Transponder

It is a combination receiver and transmitter on a satellite that relays signals transmitted to it back to earth on a different frequency.

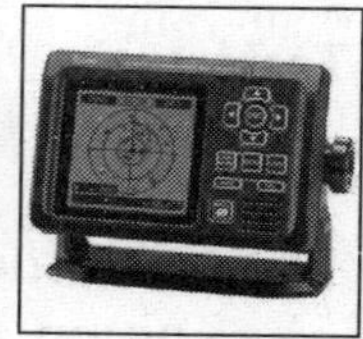

Transponder

Transport number

Another name for transference number, it is a fraction of the total current carried by a particular ion in an electrolyte.

Transuranic elements

These are radioactive elements with an atomic number greater than 92.

Transverse waves

It is defined as a wave in which disturbance is perpendicular to the direction of travel of the wave.

Travelling wave

It is the moving, periodic disturbance in a medium or field.

Triboelectricity

It is a type of static electricity created by friction in which certain materials become electrically charged after they come into contact with another different material and are then separated.

Tribiology

It is the science of the interactions between surfaces moving relative to each other. Such interactions usually involve the interplay of two primary factors: the load, or force, perpendicular to the surfaces, and the frictional force that impedes movement.

Triboluminescence

It is the emission of light by a solid substance due to mechanical damage (scratching, crashing, or grounding).

Triode

It refers to a three-element electron tube, containing a grid, cathode, and plate as active elements, in addition to the filament.

Trigonometry

It is a branch of math that deals with the relationship among angles and sides of triangles.

Triton

It is a positively charged particle consisting of a proton and two neutrons, equivalent to the nucleus of an atom of tritium.

Troposphere

It is a division of the Earth's atmosphere extending from ground level to altitudes ranging 5-10 miles.

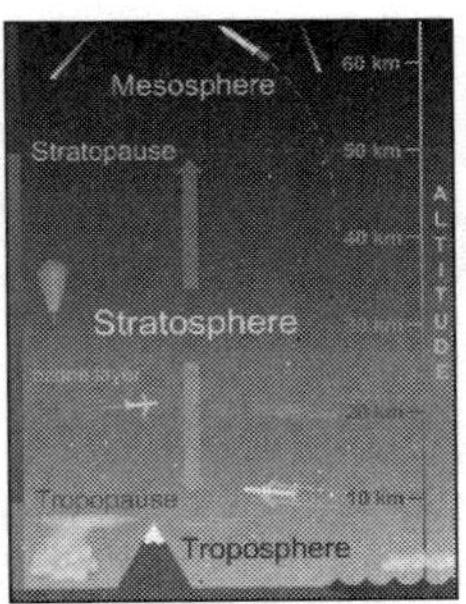

Troposphere

Trough of wave

It can be referred to as a low point of wave motion, where displacement is the most negative.

Turbine

It is a rotary engine that extracts energy from a fluid flow and converts it into useful work.

Turbogenerator

It is a combination consisting of a steam turbine and an electric generator generally on the same shaft.

Turbogenerator

Tweeter

It is a loudspeaker designed to produce high frequencies, typically from around 2,000 Hz to 20,000 Hz.

Tyndall effect

Another name for Tyndall scattering, it refers to the phenomenon in which scattering of light (mainly blue) by colloidal particles in its path takes place.

❐

U

Ultrahigh frequency

Also called the decimeter band, these are a range of electromagnetic waves with frequencies between 300 MHz and 3,000 MHz.

Ultramicroscope

This system of illumination is an optical microscope used to detect and view minute particles, which cannot be seen with ordinary microscopes, by the use of scattered light.

Ultramicroscope

Ultrasonic imaging

It is an ultrasound-based diagnostic imaging technique used to visualize subcutaneous body structures including tendons, muscles, joints, vessels, etc.

Ultrasonics

It is related to the science and application of ultrasonic waves and vibrations with a frequency above 20,000 hertz.

Ultraviolet radiation

It is an electromagnetic radiation with a wavelength shorter than that of visible light, but longer than X-rays.

Uniaxial crystal

This is a kind of crystal having one crystal axis that is different from the other two crystal axes.

Uniform acceleration

It refers to a kind of constant acceleration.

Uniform circular motion

It is a motion in a circle of constant radius with constant speed.

Unit

It refers to the unit of measurement, in which any division of quantity accepted as a standard of measurement or exchange.

Unit cell

It is the smallest group of atoms of a substance with the symmetry of a crystal, and from which the lattice can be generated by repetition in three dimensions.

Universal motor

It is an electric motor which uses electrical energy to produce mechanical energy through the interaction of magnetic fields and current-carrying conductors.

Universal motor

Universe

It is the universe is commonly defined as the totality of everything that exists, including all physical matter and energy, the planets, stars, galaxies, and the contents of intergalactic space.

Upper atmosphere

It is a layer of gases surrounding the planet Earth that is retained by Earth's gravity.

Uranium [U]

Occurring naturally in the earth's crust, this heavy, dense, toxic, silvery-grey radioactive metallic element in the actinide series with its atomic number as 92 is used for nuclear fuels and weapons.

Uranium [U]

Uranium series

Also called uranium decay series, it is the series of nuclides that begins with uranium-238 and proceeds by radioactive decay to lead-206, including isotopes of uranium, thorium, protactinium, radium, radon, etc.

V

Vacuum

It is a volume of space in which matter is absent, and its gaseous pressure is much less than atmospheric pressure.

Vacuum pump

It is a device that removes gas molecules from a sealed volume in order to leave behind a partial vacuum.

Vacuum pump

Vacuum state

It is the quantum state with the lowest possible energy.

Valence band

It can be defined as the range of energies of electrons that are bound to atoms in a solid.

Valence electrons

These are the outermost electrons of atoms, which are generally involved in bonding.

Valency

Also known as valence, it is a measure of the number of chemical bonds formed by the atoms of a given element.

Van de Graaff generator

It is an electrostatic machine that makes use of a moving belt to carry electrons to a high-voltage collector or terminal and then accelerates these charged particles to high energies.

Vapour density

It is the density of a gas relative to the density of hydrogen.

Vapour pressure

It is the particle pressure of a vapour at the surface of its parent liquid.

Variable star

It is the one whose brightness changes over time-periods ranging from minutes to years.

Variational principle

It is a scientific principle used within the calculus of variations, which develops general methods for finding functions which minimize or maximize the value of quantities that depends upon those functions.

Variometer

It is an instrument for measuring variations in the intensity of the earth's magnetic field.

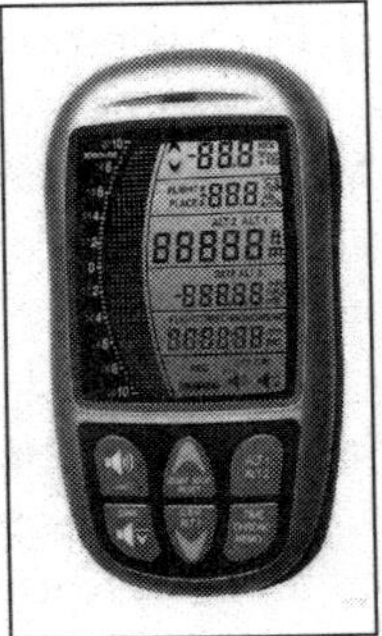

Variometer

Vector quantity

It is the quantity having both magnitude (size) and direction.

Vector resolution

It refers to a process of finding the effective value of a component in a given direction.

Velocity [symbol: v]

It means the ratio of change in position to time interval over which change takes place.

Velocity-time graph

It is a plot of velocity of object as a function of time.

Venturi tube

It is a short tube with a constricted passage that increases the velocity and lowers the pressure of a fluid conveyed through it.

Venturi tube

Vernier

It is a device permitting finer measurement or control than standard markings or adjustments.

Very high frequency

Also known as VHF, it is the radio frequency that ranges from 30 MHz to 300 MHz.

Very low frequency

Also known as VLF, it refers to the radio frequencies (RF) in the range of 3 kHz to 30 kHz.

Video camera

It is a camera used for electronic motion picture acquisition.

Virtual image

It refers to a point from which light rays appear to diverge without actually doing so.

Virtual state

It is used to refer to two different types of states in physical systems.

Virtual work

It is the work resulting from either virtual forces acting through a real displacement or real forces acting through a virtual displacement.

Viscoelasticity

It refers to the property of materials that exhibit both viscous and elastic characteristics when undergoing deformation.

Viscometer

It is an instrument for measuring the viscosity of liquids at specified temperature and atmospheric conditions.

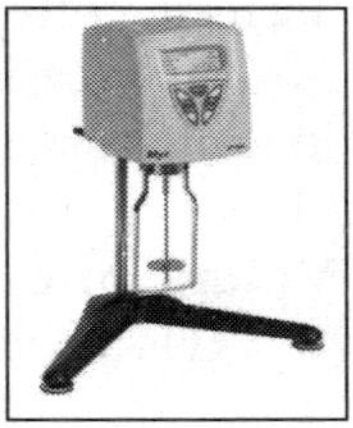

Viscometer

Viscosity

It is a measure of the resistance of a fluid which is being deformed by either shear stress or tensile stress.

Viscous fluid

It is a fluid that creates force that opposes motion of objects through it. The force is proportional to object's speed.

Visible spectrum

It refers to that portion of the electromagnetic spectrum to which the human eye is sensitive, which includes wavelengths of approximately 400 through 700 nanometers.

Volatile liquid

It is a liquid that is easily vaporized.

Volt [symbol: V]

It is the SI unit of electromotive force, the difference of potential that would drive one ampere of current against one ohm resistance.

Voltage

It is a measurement of the electromotive force in an electrical circuit or device expressed in volts.

Voltage divider

It is a series of resistors or capacitors that can be tapped at any intermediate point to produce a specific fraction of the voltage applied between its ends.

Voltaic cells

Also called galvanic cells, these are electrochemical cells in which spontaneous chemical reactions generate electricity.

Voltaic pile

It is a battery consisting of voltaic cells arranged in series.

Voltameter

Another name for coulometer, it is a scientific device, different from voltmeter, which is used for measuring and indicating the quantity of electricity.

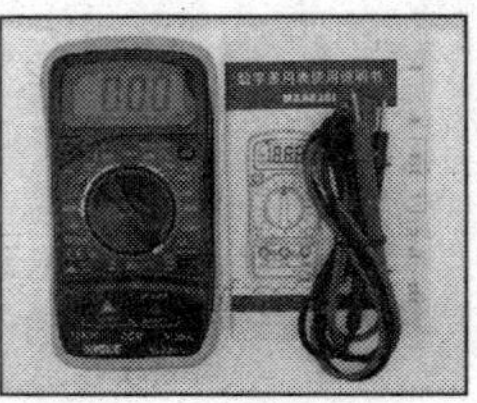

Voltmeter

Voltmeter

It is an electrical apparatus for showing the voltage of a battery or dynamo.

W

Watt

It is a unit of power, which is one joule per second.

Wattmeter

It is a kind of meter for measuring electric power in watts.

Wattmeter

Wave

It is a periodic disturbance of the particles of a substance that may be propagated without net movement of the particles, such as in the passage of undulating motion, heat, or sound.

Wave form

It refers to the shape and form of a signal such as a wave moving in a solid, liquid or gaseous medium or a vacuum.

Wave guide

It is defined as a structure which guides waves, such as electromagnetic waves or sound waves.

Wavelength

It can be defined as the distance between corresponding points on two successive waves.

Wave mechanics

It is a method of analysis of the behavior of atomic phenomena with particles represented by wave equations.

Wavemeter

It is an electrical device for measuring the wavelength of a radio frequency wave either directly or indirectly, through the determination of the frequency.

Wavemeter

Wave power

It refers to the concept of the transportation of energy by ocean surface waves, and the capture of that energy to do useful work.

Wave pulse

It is a single disturbance moving through a medium or field.

Wax

Occurring naturally as a mineral or in plants and animals, this white, translucent, moldable, solid substance, which is insoluble in water, is used in the manufacture of candles, in modelling, and polishes, etc.

Weak boson

It can be referred to as a particle that carries or transmits the weak interaction of force.

Weak electrolyte

It is a substance that conducts electricity poorly in a dilute aqueous solution.

Weak interaction

It is a force involved in beta decay of the neutron and atomic nuclei, which is one aspect of the electroweak force.

Weber [symbol: Wb]

It is the SI unit of magnetic flux, causing the electromotive force of one volt in a circuit of one turn when generated or removed in one second.

Weight

It is a force of gravity of an object.

Weightlessness

It is an object in freefall, on which only the gravitational force acts.

Weston cell

Named after Edward Weston, this standard voltaic cell generates a highly stable voltage suitable for calibration of voltmeters.

Wheatstone bridge

It is a device that measures the resistance of an electrical circuit to the flow of electricity.

Whistler

It is an atmospheric radio disturbance heard as a whistle that falls in pitch, which is usually caused by lightning.

White dwarf

It is a star that is the remnant core of a star that has completed fusion in its core.

White hole

It is a hypothetical celestial object that expands outward from a space-time singularity and emits energy, in the manner of a time-reversed black hole.

White hole

White noise

It is a noise with a continuous frequency spectrum and with equal power per unit bandwidth.

Wilson cloud chamber

It is a chamber containing supersaturated vapor through which ionizing radiation leaves trails of visible droplets.

Wind power

It is the energy generated through the use of a turbine that collects wind energy and converts it to electricity.

Wollaston prism

Named after William Hyde Wollaston, it is a prism used to obtain plane-polarized light.

Wood's metal

Also known as Lipowitz's alloy, it is a fusible, eutectic alloy consisting of bismuth plus lead, tin and cadmium.

Woofer

It is a specialized speaker that reproduces bass and lower midrange sounds.

Woofer

Work

It can be defined as a product of force and displacement in the direction of the force.

Work function

It is an energy needed to remove an electron from metal.

Work energy theorem

It can be defined as the work done on an object equal to the change in its kinetic energy.

Work hardening

Also called strain hardening, it refers to the strengthening of a material by repeated plastic deformation, resulting in a distortion of its crystal structure.

World line

It is a path in spacetime, especially that traversed by an elementary particle from its creation to its destruction.

World Wide Web

Abbreviated as WWW, it is a system of interlinked hypertext documents accessed via the Internet.

Wrought iron

Wrought iron

Made by puddling pig iron when molten, it is a tough, malleable kind of iron with low carbon content, which is used mainly as a building material.

❒

X-ray astronomy

It is the branch of astronomy concerned with the detection and measurement of high-energy electromagnetic radiation emitted by celestial objects.

X-ray crystallography

It is the study of crystals and their structure by means of X-ray diffraction.

X-ray diffraction

It is the scattering of X-rays by the regularly spaced atoms of a crystal, useful in obtaining information about the structure of the crystal.

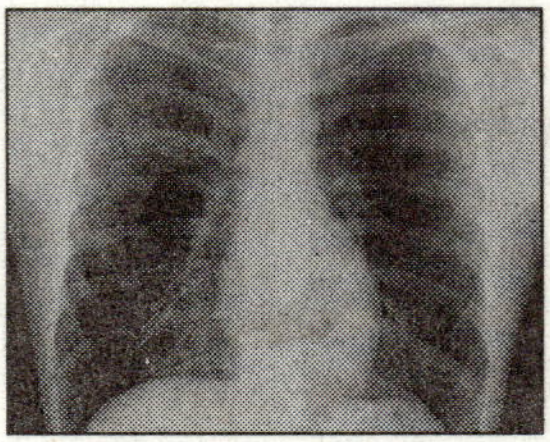

X-rays

It is a form of electromagnetic radiation of short wavelength (in the range of 0.01 to 10 nanometers).

X-rays

X-ray diffraction

It refers to a complicated technique using x-rays to "create an image" where no lens to focus the light rays is available.

X-ray images

These are images such as photographs or computer enhanced images produced by bombarding a target with x-rays.

X-ray tube

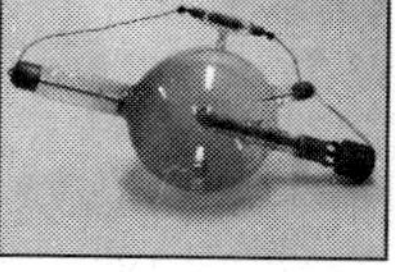

X-ray tube

It is a device for generating X-rays by accelerating electrons to high energies and causing them to strike a metal target from which the X-rays are emitted.

❐

Y

Yagi aerial

It refers to a sharply directional antenna.

Yard

It is a unit of linear measure equal to 3 feet (0.9144 meter).

Year

It is the time taken by a planet to make one revolution around the sun, which includes the period of 365 days.

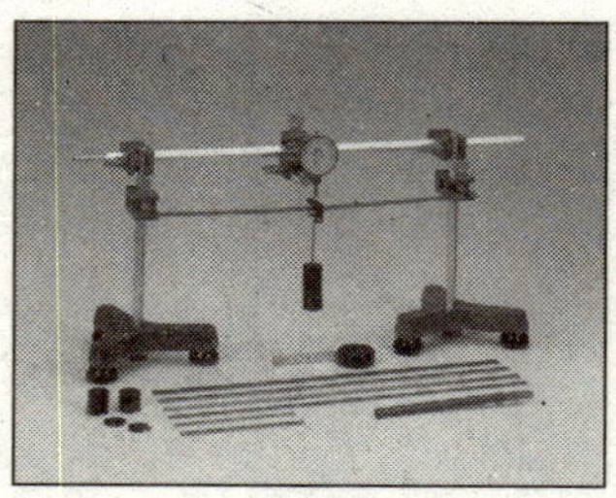

Young's modulus

Young's modulus

It is a constant of proportionality associated with the change in length of a material according to its elastic properties.

❑

Zener diode

It is a diode that allows reverse current to flow above a set voltage limit, and is usually used as a voltage regulator.

Zenith

It refers to the point on the celestial sphere vertically above the observer.

Zero-point energy

It is the lowest energy state of molecular vibration.

Zodiac

It is an imaginary belt circling the heavens, including the paths of the sun, moon, and major planets, and containing twelve constellations.

Zodiacal light

It is a faint cone of light that can sometimes be seen above the horizon after sunset or before sunrise.

Zodiacal light

Zone refining

It is a technique of purifying a bar of metal by passing it through an induction heater.

Zoom lens

It is an optical system of continuously variable focal length with the focal plane remaining in a fixed position.

Zoom lens

Zwitterions

These are dipolar ions that contain positive and negative charges of equal strength, and are therefore not attracted to either anode or cathode.